Indian Business Case Studies

Indian Business Case Studies

Volume VII

VARSHA PARAB

RAMESH MAHADIK

DIKSHA TRIPATHI

Indian Case Studies in Business Management

OXFORD
UNIVERSITY PRESS

OXFORD
UNIVERSITY PRESS

Great Clarendon Street, Oxford, ox2 6dp,
United Kingdom

Oxford University Press is a department of the University of Oxford.
It furthers the University's objective of excellence in research, scholarship,
and education by publishing worldwide. Oxford is a registered trade mark of
Oxford University Press in the UK and in certain other countries

© ASM Group of Institutes, Pune, India 2022

The moral rights of the authors have been asserted

Impression: 1

DISCLAIMER: ASM Group of Institutes and the Series Editors including the Individual Volume Authors of the Title **Indian Business Studies Volumes** hereby declare that the business Case Studies in the title are developed and as included in this Case Volume are based on Information, event details and the names of protagonists, issues, the tables and graphic representations are from published data available in public domain as appearing in daily national and/or regional news media. There are no sensitive issues included in the contents of the Titles and there are no Intensions to hurt any Professional/Business/Religious/Social sentiments of individuals, society or organizations and any regulative machinery.

Published in the United States of America by Oxford University Press
198 Madison Avenue, New York, NY 10016, United States of America

British Library Cataloguing in Publication Data

Data available

Library of Congress Cataloging-in-Publication Data: 2022938091

ISBN 978-0-19-286943-2

DOI: 10.1093/oso/9780192869432.001.0001

Printed in India by
Rakmo Press Pvt. Ltd.

Links to third party websites are provided by Oxford in good faith and
for information only. Oxford disclaims any responsibility for the materials
contained in any third party website referenced in this work.

Group of Institutions to a higher position of leadership that be world-class and internationally ranked at business management.

Dr R.R. Pachpande
[1947–2009]

'Education is the Soul of our society'

The series editors and the volume authors of the Case Volumes Titled as 'Indian Business Case Studies', published by Oxford University Press, have a deep sense of gratefulness while dedicating these Case Volumes to the memory of Dr Raghunath R. Pachpande, the founder of ASM Group of Institutes, Pune, India

It was with the untiring efforts and Strategic Vision of Dr R.R. (as he was known to his close friends and colleagues) which has been instrumental in ASM Group adopting case methodology as a unique element in its pedagogy which motivated the faculty and students of ASM Group of Institutes to develop business case studies on Indian businesses and use them to teach management subjects in all branches of business management studies.

Dr R.R. Pachpande was a leader beyond parlance and ahead of time in establishing educational institutes, more so in higher studies in business management, specifically in the industrial belts in the state of Maharashtra with a view to providing the best of experiential learning to its students through closer interactions with business units around.

Today, ASM Group continues the great legacy of Dr R.R. Pachpande under the leadership of his successors and who have succeeded in taking ASM

Group to global recognition as a unique group of institutes offering world-class education in all branches of business management.

This Case Volume is dedicated to the memories of the late Dr R.R. Pachpande.

Contents

SECTION II CASE STUDIES IN FINANCE MANAGEMENT

SECTION III MULTIDISCIPLINARY CASE STUDIES IN MARKETING, STRATEGY, OPERATIONS

Preface

Many universities and management institutes across the globe have adopted the case study methodology for teaching almost all branches of management studies for several decades. This trend has been seen in India also, wherein the Indian Institutes of Management (IIMs) and progressive management institutes in the private sector have implemented case methodology as an important pedagogical tool in business management education.

However, there is a severe shortage in Indian business case studies faced by the B-schools in India and those global institutes associated with Indian academia. The majority of the case studies studied at IIMs and other A-grade B-schools in India are from situations in industries in foreign countries and have very little or no relevance to Indian business situations. This acts as a major gap for faculty and student engagement in business management studies both at UG and masters level (PG) studies, wherein for clarification of theoretical concepts is possible mainly through f use of case methodology, which enables insight into business real-life business situations.

Besides, the objectives and purposes for which case studies are developed abroad are much different from the course of studies in Indian B-schools. Therefore, the dependence on foreign case studies for Indian students does not provide any real situational insight into Indian business. Although the curriculum requires taking the students through case study methodology, there are not many Indian case studies for this purpose.

The main objectives of using case-based teaching as a major pedagogical tool in B-schools are as follows:

1. To facilitate students' concept development capabilities through exposure to real-life problems in industries

2. To enable students to correlate theoretical topics with the techniques used in analysing complex issues in business situations

3. To develop skills using which students can develop application matrix for the theoretical topics for real-life problem analysis and resolution techniques

4. Help the students of B-schools to develop orientation towards the important attributes and attitudinal requirements for effective handling of complex situations at the workplace

5. To develop a clear understanding of the techniques used for problem analysis, situation analysis, and decision analysis and appropriate understanding of the difference between problems and situations in management

6. To develop the group-based approaches to solving problems and challenges at the workplace by appropriate coordination of and collaboration with all related aspects of a situation

7. To develop a reference manual for recording the problems tackled and the essential lessons learnt from past incidences for use in future eventualities of recurrence of issues

8. To develop the preventive steps that must be initiated to ensure the problems resolved once do not recur in the immediate future

Business case studies are basically oriented towards developing the evaluative and analytical skills of students towards industry situations. Such case studies draw the attention of participants of the case resolution methodology on the in-depth correlative evaluation of the issues in the case study with the various related topics that the students have to study about in their classrooms. These case studies could be on issues related to human resources, industrial relations, product and process, marketing, and finance management areas in business management.

The academic environment across the world, too, is facing a major disruption on account of the global pandemic COVID 19, forcing the offline education system to switch over to online/blended versions of the teaching and learning process. And the use of case methodology and simulation exercises are the main in gradients for sustaining effective ways of delivering experiential learning through the use of case and case lets in an online mode of teaching, ensuring student engagements and online interactive ways of knowledge dissemination.

Oxford University Press, in association with ASM Group of Institutes Pune, India, is publishing for the first time a comprehensive Case Volumes as series of eight volumes with case studies on Indian Businesses selected from all aspects of business functions like HR, finance marketing, and operations, and providing an exciting and long waited opportunity to faculty and students across the globe to access Indian business case studies through these Case Volumes.

We are very confident that the Case Volumes will receive a very good response and will be of utmost use to the readers.

Acknowledgements

The series editors wish to acknowledge with thanks the contribution of data for the case studies from ASM's Academic Associates, the CETYS University Mexico—Dr Scott Venezia, Dean International Affairs, and Dr Francisco Velez Dean of Colleges, CETYS as also several senior faculties from ASM Group of Institutes for their help in contributing case studies for the Case Volumes.

We also acknowledge the numerous news reporters of daily newspapers in business and economics in India, which have been rich and authentic secondary data sources for the design and development of case studies for the Case Volumes.

The How and Why of Case Methodology

An insight into the use of Case Methodology in B-school pedagogy.

Case Methodology in Business Management Studies

The main objectives of using case-based teaching as a major pedagogical tool in B-schools are as follows:

1. To facilitate students' concept development capabilities through exposure to real-life problems in industries
2. To enable students to correlate theoretical topics with the techniques used in analysing complex issues in business situations
3. To develop skills using which students can develop application matrix for the theoretical topics for real-life problem analysis and resolution techniques

4. Help the students of B-schools to develop orientation towards the important attributes and attitudinal requirements for effective handling of complex situations at the workplace
5. To develop a clear understanding of the techniques used for problem analysis, situation analysis, and decision analysis and an appropriate understanding of the difference between problems and situations in management
6. To develop the group-based approaches to solving problems and challenges at the workplace by appropriate coordination of and collaboration with all related aspects of a situation
7. To develop a reference manual for recording the problems tackled and the essential lessons learnt from past incidences for use in future eventualities of recurrence of issues
8. To develop the preventive steps that must be initiated to ensure the problems resolved once do not recur in the immediate future

Major Types of Case Studies

The entire gamut of business case studies can be classified as follows:

1. Evaluative case studies (teaching case studies)
2. Task- or action-oriented case studies (including project-based case studies)
3. Research-oriented case studies

Evaluative or teaching case studies are basically oriented towards developing the evaluative and analytical skills of students towards industry situations. Such case studies draw the attention of participants of the case resolution methodology on the in-depth correlative evaluation of the issues in the case study with the various related topics that the students have to study about in their classrooms.

These case studies could be on issues related to human resources, industrial relations, product and process, marketing, and finance management areas in business management. Such case studies help the students mainly to examine their understanding of evaluative steps such as evaluation of the financial situation of a company or the quality aspects of its products and services, etc.

The task- or action-oriented case studies dwell on business issues that call for appropriate decision-making capabilities of executives. By involving students of management studies in the resolution activity of such case studies, the skills learnt by them through the theoretical studies can be experimented in the resolution exercises. The students can be motivated to apply their decision-making skills along with their risk management ability to make business decisions.

Developing a plan of actions oriented towards the resolution of the case issues calls for effective role-play techniques as also presentation skills from the part of students; they are normally required to defend their plan of approach and decisions in front of other students and the faculty, which helps them improve their capabilities to sustain questions and criticisms, normal features in business management.

Research-based case studies, as the name suggests, involve students in research initiatives to establish a hypothesis or to disprove a common belief, which influence the progress and sustenance of business ideologies or even scientific or technical aspects of business dynamics.

These case studies normally call for prerequisites such as thorough business knowledge and enough exposure to both the theoretical and practical aspects of the issues presented in the case studies. Issues of corporate governance and social welfare functions, which have both obligatory and voluntary elements attached to them, are pursued in research studies to establish the utility purposes of such aspects, which range from free will to a compelled activity.

Market-survey case studies help students to differentiate between facts and fantasies of customer behaviour and understand the competitive forces at play in the marketplace. Business environmental analysis and the study of business options and strategic choices are recommended areas for case studies calling for research.

However, the real problem today for B-schools is the non-availability of good case studies on Indian business. Since the usage of imported case studies from foreign businesses is fast losing its relevance to the Indian business scenario, which in itself has unique features among the global economies. India, which is rated as the world's fourth-largest economy, definitely needs specific and separate approaches to the case study methodology as a pedagogical tool for B-school studies.

This also calls for intensifying the industry–institute interactions at least at the B-school level of education. Both sides need to shed their shy or protective nature to facilitate effective and purposeful interactions.

Even the government, and specifically the department of higher education, needs to emphasize the absolute need for closer contacts between the higher educational institutes and the business houses in all segments of the economy. Only then can the studies at higher level be compatible with the needs of businesses, and the educational degrees or qualifications be worthy of any application in the real economic progress of India, based on domestic skills as relevant to business needs.

Case studies in business management are characterized by their relevance to the theories and practices of businesses across the world. While there could be cultural differentiation, the need is to align with the basic purpose of business ventures. Men, machines, and materials form the basic resources of a business, and customers at the relevant marketplace create the necessary turnover of these resources.

Every business or entrepreneurial venture is preceded by the necessity of there being means for survival and creation of wealth by the stakeholders. It is in a way a mixture of needs, actions, and results in a perpetual series and cycle of events, which consume and recreate themselves for the continuity of life on this planet perhaps.

Case Study: Design and Development Methodology

Case studies in business management are characterized by their relevance to the theories and practices of businesses across the world. While there could be cultural differentiation, the need is to align with the basic purpose of business ventures. Men, machines, and materials form the basic resources of a business, and customers at the relevant marketplace create the necessary turnover of these resources.

Every business or entrepreneurial venture is preceded by the necessity of there being means for survival and creation of wealth by the stakeholders. It is in a way a mixture of needs, actions, and results in a perpetual series and cycle of events, which consume and recreate themselves for the continuity of life on this planet perhaps.

The case studies in business management depend very much on the 'virtual' nature of their contents, and the actual and real-life demonstration of business situations that they bring to the classroom in business schools help in letting the students correlate the theoretical and practical aspects of business management.

Case studies should generate interest in the minds of students and awake in them a curiosity to understand the contents of a case study and an urge to involve oneself in the case analysis and resolution process. Then only can case studies be called effective tools that translate real-life business scenarios to classroom discussion topics.

The case studies in business management are characterized by features as follows:

1. Fact-based contents and narrations rather than fantasies and fiction.
2. Necessity of an appropriate 'hook effect' in case contents and the chronological presentation of a case.
3. Presence of just enough ambiguity and vagueness in the deliberations of the case.
4. Providing clues and not exact solutions to case issues.
5. Providing specificity in the comparison and correlation of case contents to topics of studies in business management.

Case Study based on Facts

In order to make a case study present a real-life situation, it should necessarily be based on the facts of a business situation, either a past situation or a concurrent happening in the domestic or international business environment. However, in order to protect an individual's or an organization's business interests, one may, to the maximum extent possible, camouflage the names of individuals, organizations, or the exact product and process nomenclatures, besides duly respecting the copyrights of the owners of the references made, if any, in the case contents.

The students of business management definitely desire to feel involved when they have to study, analyse and resolve business case studies; hence, any distortion in the facts, details not confirming to regular business transactions or issues not commonly visualized during the course of their studies tend to deflect their focus and create a sense of artificiality or disinterest in their approach to the case study methodology.

In fact, this is one of the most important reasons why case studies based on industrial situations abroad are of lesser interest to the students of Indian B-schools, since they do not depict real business scenarios in the Indian business environment and are deprived of the cultural relevance so essential to Indian students.

It is also observed that in many case studies, an attempt is made by the authors of the case study to dramatize the narration to such an extent that the seriousness of the topic in relation to business management studies is completely disregarded. And such case studies are remembered by the students for their fun content rather than facts of business life. This has an implied risk in that students may totally miss the objective of the case study methodology of business management studies and consider case studies as irrelevant to business studies' requirements.

A good case study, therefore, should necessarily draw the attention of students to the events and facts normally reported in the business magazines or based on reports appearing in the newspapers, a journal, such that the students' natural interests are aroused to know more about the issues involved through case analysis and discussions. Students who are aware of the happenings in the business world around them will be happy to clarify their understanding of the theoretical aspects of their course of management studies by making the best use of case study methodology.

Necessity of 'Hook Effect' in Business Case Studies

For a film to be entertaining and interesting till the last scene, it must capture the imagination of the audience and make them feel as though they are a part of the environment created by the film; similarly, it is necessary that business case studies create a feeling in the students that they are a part of the case study from the beginning to the final resolution. This is the essential hook effect that every case study in business management should strive to achieve.

Mind well that this does not mean the authors should resort to fantasizing the narration of case contents; the purpose of films is pure entertainment, whereas the purpose of business case studies is to develop a strong sense of attachment of the student towards case contents, as is relevant to their course of studies; it is in their own interests to understand the analysis and resolution process of a particular case study that looks so similar to real-life business situations about which they have some knowledge.

Case studies in business management should provide enough opportunities for conflicts and disagreements, lively discussions, and competitive team spirit among the students. The case studies should also generate an interest in the students to look out for additional data from sources such as the Internet and business magazines, balance sheets of companies, etc., to gather further information to help them understand management concepts and prepare them to provide effective analysis and resolutions to the questions raised by the case writer.

Every business executive necessarily suffers much anxiety and related stressful situations in the resolution of day-to-day problems at the workplace. The purpose of business case studies is to simulate an environment that is as real as possible using the case content and analysis and resolution process.

'Ambiguity and Vagueness' in Business Cases

A professional manager often comes across ambiguous and vague situations including discontinuous changes in their day-to-day activities. In fact, these situations incite creative and innovative responses from the managers, leading to ensuring sustainability amidst volatile market forces. If every step is based on logic and must be preplanned or doctored, then perhaps life will not be worth living it.

In the parlance of strategic management, we often talk of change management and of 'discontinuous changes', which defy logic and sense of sequencing of events. The real capability factors for effective business management are the ones that can manage business uncertainties like never before in globalized competitive environments. It is these uncertainties, which are the real ambiguities and vagueness in business management, that the case studies are supposed to imbibe while the students are on the lookout for logical steps in analysis and issue resolution.

Case studies should induce the students to think outside the box for the resolution of issues for a given situation. A case study should not be a drab story from the cradle to the grave or a reincarnation of business practices, which kills the creative capabilities of students and oversimplifies the challenges faced in effective business management. The case studies should deflect logic-based thinking to change management areas wherein the students are required to play different roles in providing long-term solutions to the issues mentioned in the case studies. Questions such as why, when, how, how much, who, etc., should naturally surface while analysing and resolving case issues.

'Clues' for Case Analysis and Resolution

Providing clues and soft hints along the sequence of events in case study analysis and resolution will enable students to direct their analyses towards the objectives of the case study. It is often the experience that students lose their focus on important aspects of the case study and start drifting towards issues on less critical points.

This is also quite often the case in real-life industry situations wherein the major focus in important discussions gets deflected to trivial issues, resulting in wastage of valuable time, conflicts of interests, and escalation of the problem rather than arriving at any resolution. Business case studies should make special attempts to keep the focus of the analysis and resolution methodology oriented on major issues.

This can be done by proper sequencing of events in the case study such that the readers of the case are provided with links to the theme of the case as frequently as required by providing clues to the root causes for the issues and hints to the likely solution or answers to the questions asked by the case writer.

For example, if the case writer wants the students to compare the case issues with 'competitive strategy' situations, then the mention of 'competitive environment' as an often-repeated data or issue in the case study would keep the students focused in their analysis and discussions on, say, the 'competitive advantage matrix', as enumerated by Michel Porter on strategic business management topics.

Similarly, case studies in human resources (HR) should provide clues on HR-related issues, rather than constantly talking about competition and product-related issues. Of course, in the case of case studies in overall operations management including mergers and acquisitions, it would be prudent to provide related clues on each functional area and the respective topics in classroom studies.

Nevertheless, should the clues attempt to mislead the participants, the very belief and credibility of the case study methodology of studies would be destroyed. It is also equally important to note that the clues should only be indicative and not directive in their purpose.

Case Teaching Notes

Case study teaching notes are primarily for the case instructor or the faculty who use the case study methodology for teaching business management topics to students. Following are some of the important aspects of case teaching notes (these are not exclusive in their coverage; the concerned faculty could add, delete or modify the same to make their case teaching process as effective as possible):

Every case presenter should provide students with a brief summary of the case in order to generate initial awareness and prepare the students to study the case as a cursory note or a preamble of their expectations from the analysis and resolution efforts required for the case study.

A list of the main topic and sub-topics intended to be taught through the particular case study needs to be prepared and discussed beforehand by the faculty with the students, in order to ensure there is enough clarity of understanding and expectations from a particular case study.

Reference to important theories such as Maslow's theory, Herz Berg's theory, Michel Porter's model on business competitive and market forces, GE 9 cell model for investment decisions, etc., in any other specialization area of business management studies should be made in a separate 'Focus of Studies' part of the teaching notes and should be shared with the students in advance of case study discussions to enable the students to consolidate their understanding and applicability of a particular theory during the analysis and resolution process of case study discussions.

The teaching notes should also contain corollary topics and references to other aspects of the course of studies, which may not have been covered in the main case content. Additional information about a product, process, or business unit or comparisons with similar real-life situations and relevant market situations, if available with the faculty, is shared with the concerned students; this will help the students to correlate their knowledge with this additional information, which refers to an actual situation.

Every faculty should necessarily collect feedback from the groups or individuals who have studied the case and their comments on the utility of the case study towards their course of business management studies must be noted. This feedback will help the faculty to make necessary improvements in leading the case study by answering certain observations made by the participants.

Every faculty should prepare an assignment case study to be completed by the students, to encourage students to experience the work-life through exercises in case study resolutions.

Prevalent Methods for Case Analysis and Resolution

Case study methods used for providing clarity on management concepts mostly focus on either imaginary situations or events based on records of failures or successes in the organizational setup. Besides, the approach for case-studies resolution has often focused merely on 'SWOT' analysis (SWOT stands for strengths, weaknesses, opportunities, and threats involved in a project) of an organization with a lesser degree of focus on failures in areas such as strategic decision making, strategic planning, and compatibility in organizations to strategic approach and implementation. The issues in strategically managed companies basically emanate from weaknesses in strategic thinking and a systematic approach to problem resolution.

As Dr Peter Drucker, the management guru, says: 'Management of many business units are busy resolving yesterday's problems today. And there is hardly any clarity between problems and opportunity'. He continues: 'Business investments for competitive advantage need to focus on investments in opportunities rather than in problems'. It is observed that many business organizations take comfort in handing over to the consultants the real problems of the organization. In the first instance, there is no reason for problems to exist if one is to ensure strategic correction during the implementation of strategies in ongoing or new business ventures.

The consultants, in many cases, help expedite the early death of such businesses with their third-party approach (lack of involvement and commitment) to the issues referred and their practice of extracting hefty charges for their consultancy reports, most of which are vague prescriptions (glorified 'sounds good'-type recommendations) that help boardrooms feel happy that their future is secured.

However, in today's globalized competitive business environment, the top management needs to lay special emphasis on attending present issues, focusing on the resolution of present issues, burying past problems with appropriate strategy implementation and preparing for the future, which calls for competitive advantage capabilities.

Further, many companies like business process outsourcing (BPO) companies, knowledge process outsourcing (KPO) companies, and multinational companies (MNCs) are under the clutches of the managerial autocratic ('do as we say') approach. This reduces the creativity of their employees and converts them to mere 'robots' in their attitudes and presentations. Today, from middle school to management studies, logic-based computer-aided business planning processes are being emphasized rather than creativity-enhancing involvements that call for human endeavour in attaining success and satisfaction.

Understanding the major working details of any organization entails the collection of relevant data from sources such as present status and past records of organizational health. In the majority of cases, we need to analyse the past performance data. As in the case of biological issues, in an organizational life history, there are events and episodes that occur as major factors inhibiting the progress or causing the decline of the organization; in such cases, often the management had no clue or controlling authority over the organization to understand the issues or prevent the decline in advance.

Diagnosing these maladies affecting an organization is comparable to a doctor conducting a diagnostic investigation into the serious ailments of his or her patient. For serious ailments (excepting epidemics and contagious diseases), all factors and issues that influence the malady are personal habits, malnutrition, hygiene factors, and also immunity factors developed during the past period that are either protective or provocative to health or sickness, respectively.

Case History—Details

1. Symptoms: Present and past, as recorded.
2. Historical data: Business past history, including all important factors such as details of promoters, financing, products, prices, and marketing.
3. Factors influencing performance:
   a. Congenital factors: Family background (erstwhile business promoters, vision, mission, and objectives); any effects of 'success sclerosis' (arrogance due to affluence from past success), or 'points of inflection' as is called in business terms, could be factors that go unrecognized in the present malady.
   b. Professionalization and management thoughts on fresh approach, skill building, and competence factors: These lead to the restless urge to change over from complacence to competence (in a competitive market situation) or from intolerance to the infectivity of people and processes (as compared to the 'we too ran' attitude of the organization in the past).
   c. As in the case of diversification or acquisition and mergers, the issues could result from correct or defective selection of businesses (products and processes) or partners, the necessity to change, consequent changes in management capability, improvement anxiety syndrome, etc.
   d. Hurdles in succession planning: The 'Generation Next' may have different value systems (sometimes non-compatible with those of its predecessors) and not have a balanced or matured approach as seen by business observers.

e. Fresh approach to business philosophy, a new vision or mission in light of the changing global economy: Both vertical and horizontal integrations (forward and backward integrations) aid typical expectations of the customers of the emancipated market environment.

f. Inability to tolerate the impact of coexistence of new and old cultures.

The following logical, sequential, and important steps help to understand, in a comprehensive manner, analysis and resolutions for a case study of any type of business or industry at both corporate and functional levels:

1. Data collection and segmentation (case details)
2. Discuss issues/dilemmas/problems involved in the case
3. Diagnosis (case analysis): Correlating issues of the case with relevant styles of narration in terms of management terminology, in practical business life and conducting a SWOT analysis if required
4. Case resolution (issue resolution—resolutions and recommendations)
   a. Short term (intermediate steps): Damage control steps
   b. Long term (back to life): Regaining normal health
   c. Preventive steps (impact of implementing the recommendations)
      i. Consequent prevention-oriented recommendations
      ii. Building strategic capabilities in subjects (organization) to develop the capability to succeed and develop adequate immunity in case the challenge or malady repeats or has side effects in an altogether new dimension
5. Record of lessons learnt
   a. Appropriate record of cause-and-effect analysis of issues
   b. Record of probability analysis

Serial Number	Case History (Major Details)	Disease (Investigative Observation) Issues (Major) of the Case	Diagnosis (Relevance to Management Terminology)	Treatment		Preventive Measures (Prepared for Consequences, if Any)	Lesson Learnt (Case Record for Future Reference)
				Short Term	Long Term		

Stages/Areas of Activity	Tools Recommended
Strategy formulation	Vision, mission, objective orientation driver/business drivers/critical success factors
Strategic analysis	Environmental appraisal methods:
	Direct–indirect
	Macro–micro
	External–internal stake Holders
	Organizational appraisal methods:
	SWOT analysis
	Risk analysis
	Boston Consultancy Group matrix
	GE 9 cell model
	For investment decisions
Strategic options	Acceptability
	Feasibility
	Flexibility
Strategic choice	Best choice matrix
	Must/wish drill
Strategic decisions	Decision matrix
	Decision tree
	Short- and long-term impact analyses
Strategy implementation	Operational control method
	Strategic control method

Stages/Areas of Activity	Tools Recommended
Strategy evaluation	Gap analysis
	Root cause analysis
	Probability factor analysis of present and potential effects
	Corrective steps
	Review progress
	Reconfirm strategic alignment

The case studies included in this Case Volume VII are selected diligently to provide a very variety of businesses and issues involved in each of the cases being much different than the other. The chapters cover almost all types and segments of industry and markets, providing a very good opportunity for the readers to refer to the aspects explained in this brief note on case methodology and its utility in concept clarification and exposure to experiential learning for the students of B-schools as also to younger business executives up the career ladder.

About the Series Editors

Dr Sandeep Pachpande, Chairman,
ASM Group of Institutes, Pune, India

Prof J. A. Kulkarni, Professor,
ASM Group of Institutes, Pune, India

Both the series editors have decades of experience in business case design and development and also implementation of case methodology of teaching for the faculty and students of business schools in India and abroad.

The series editors have to their credit for authoring three major books on business case studies published by globally known publishers and in conducting workshops for case design and development.

The series editors have a very good network with leaders and stalwarts in business management studies across the globe and are popular as keynote speakers in many national and international conferences. They have a very rich experience in organizing national and international conferences and case competitions.

Currently, the series editors are busy completing a unique case analysis and resolution methodology program which is under copyright considerations.

Dr Sandeep Pachpande

Prof J. A. Kulkarni

About the Volume Authors

Prof Ramesh Mahadik
M Tech (Computer Science and Engineering)

He is currently engaged as Professor at Institute of Management and Computer Science & Technology—IMCOST, ASM Group of Institutes, Mumbai, India.

Key Executive Management Skills

• **Managing Operations**	• **Team Building/Motivation**
• Business Development	• Competency Building
• Building Training Strategies	• Forming Strategic Alliances
• Implementation of Systems and Processes	• Driving Innovation

Research Papers Published

1. Expert System for Diagnosis of Pulmonary Disorders
2. Business Intelligence for SMEs and Review of Three Open Source BI Tools
3. Deciphering Big Data Analytics
4. Internet of Things (IoT)—Architectural Elements, Applications, and Challenges
5. Technology Integration and Adoption in Education
6. A Conceptual Overview of Machine Learning and Its Applications
7. An Overview of Blockchain Tech and Its Applications

Dr Varsha Parab
MMS, MBA, PhD

Dr Varsha Parab has nearly three decades of professional experience both in industry and academics and has established herself as a senior-level faculty and in guiding the students not only in management studies but equally moulding the students for improved employability credentials.

Dr Varsha has presented research papers in national and international conferences as also in organizing and conducting case competitions for faculty, students, and corporate executives.

Dr Diksha Tripathi
B.Com, MBA, PhD (Finance)

Dr Diksha Tripathi has 10 years of rich experience and worked as senior faculty in reputed management institutes with expertise in finance management and more so in the adoption of business case methodology.

Diksha Tripathi provides excellent inputs as a senior faculty in finance management both in offline and online teaching and learning techniques.

Dr Tripathi has authored many research papers presented in national and international conferences and published major articles in text and reference books. In particular, major case studies as authored by Dr

Tripathi have been included in Case Volumes and case competitions held in India and abroad.

Presently, Dr Diksha Tripathi is engaged as Professor at ASM Institute of Business Management and Research.

SECTION I

CASE STUDIES IN HUMAN RESOURCES

1

Employee Unrest and the Role of Labour Unions

A Case Study of Indian SME

Learning Objectives

To understand the business strategy to fulfil the demand of employees/ workers. To understand the real problem of the company from employee perspectives. To lead towards the right direction by analysing the current labour union of the SMEs. To understand different factors which can help resolving issues. Strategic decision-making.

Synopsis

Four engineers formed a group and started a small and medium enterprise (SME) in 1975 in the vicinity of Mumbai. Their activity was manufacturing of vessels of Mild Steel (MS), Stainless Steel (SS) material required for pharmaceuticals, chemical companies, fertilizer companies, large government and private enterprises like Hindustan Oil Corporation (HOC), National Organic and Chemicals India Limited (NOCIL), Hardllia Chemicals, Standard Alkalie, and other dairy and pharmacy companies. The total strength of the company was more than 500 workers. In 1978, workers formed a union. Due to the financial crisis, this company was not in a position to consider the demands with 25 items. Later on, two unions formed under two different leaders. Finally, in the 1980s, Mr. Kishor Salvi received a certificate of recognition in 'Dish Ends Ltd' and then the settlement took place by accepting 20 demands out of 25

Indian Business Case Studies. Varsha Parab, Ramesh Mahadik, and Diksha Tripathi, Oxford University Press.
© ASM Group of Institutes, Pune, India 2022. DOI: 10.1093/oso/9780192869432.003.0001

original demands under Maharashtra Recognition of Trade Unions and Prevention of Unfair Labour Laws Practices (MRTU and PULP) Act 1971.

Historical Relevance

MRTU and PULP Act 1971 sanctioned by the Government of India for regulations of industries in the country to attain the goal of empathy between employee and employer. This act figures on the incidence of the strike, lockout, illegally declared, economizing, terminating a workman. Under such circumstances, the Industrial Act can be closely related and several other problems between employee and employer. In such unwanted industry issues, the Industrial Act, MRTU and PULP Act 1971 against Unfair Labour Practices (ULPs) are provided.

The MRTU and PULP Act 1971 Preamble to Maharashtra Act no. i of 1972:

> An Act to provide for the recognition of trade unions for facilitating col-lective bargaining for certain undertakings, to state their rights, and obli-gations; to confer certain powers on Unrecognized unions; to provide for declaring certain strikes and lock-outs as illegal strikes and lock-outs; to define and provide for the prevention of certain unfair labour practices; to constitute courts (as independent machinery) for carrying out the pur-poses of according recognition to trade unions and for enforcing the pro-visions relating to unfair practices; and to provide for matters connected with the purposes aforesaid. WHEREAS, by Government Resolution, Industries and Labour Department, No. IDA. 1367-LAB-II, dated the 14th February 1968, the Government of Maharashtra appointed a Committee called 'the Committee on Unfair Labour Practices' for defining certain activities of employers and workers and their organ-izations which should be treated as unfair labour practices and for sug-gesting action which should be taken against employers or workers, or their organizations, for engaging in such unfair labour practices; AND
>
> WHEREAS, after taking into consideration the report of the Committee Government is of opinion that it is expedient to provide for the recognition of trade unions for facilitating collective bargaining for certain undertakings; to state their rights and obligations; to confer

certain powers on Unrecognized unions; to provide for declaring certain strikes and lock-outs as illegal strikes and lock-outs; to define and provide for the prevention of certain unfair labour practices; to constitute courts (as independent machinery) for carrying out the purposes of according recognition to trade unions and for enforcing provisions relating to unfair practices; and to provide for matters connected with the purposes aforesaid. (IDA 1367-LAB-II)

In the year 1970, there was a boom in the industrial revolution in India. The law completely favours employees' demands. But due to leadership issues, the management of the company always takes the benefit of different leaders by keeping a different relationship with two different leaders. Almost two decades due to disputes between two union companies could not give principal benefits to the employee as they demanded at the beginning of the company's establishment.

Importance of SMEs

SMEs are extremely important to any economy. Even more critical for developing countries like India where the gap between the rich and the poor is increasing day by day and not to forget the headache of unemployment. The recent Oxfam survey stated the same when it mentioned about how a minimum wage worker in rural India will take 941 years to earn the equivalent of the top paid executive in a garment firm.

SMEs contribute to the Indian economy not only by participating in the development of the mainstream economy but also by creating some 'decent' jobs. From Dudley Seers to Amartya Sen, everybody has emphasized that for the economic development of the country, three factors must be taken into consideration: reducing the (1) poverty, (2) inequality, and (3) unemployment. SMEs are of key importance to the Indian economy.

Be it the government's policies supporting and encouraging the SMEs growth, like Make in India, Startup India, and Skill India, these policies and programs have been implemented to boost the SMEs growth by the Indian government. At the same time, the government's other focus area—Digital India is also helping the small players get aligned with m-payments and e-commerce. While the SMEs are trying to grow their business, and with the government working on contributing to the same goal, the new fintech sector has come up and around very rapidly. Fintech start-ups are helping in improving the SME lending for the SMEs. For all their Investment, for modernisation and expansion projects.

Outcomes

In any SME, there should not be two labour unions. If more than one labour union is formed by the employee, they will not be in a position to get employee benefits from the management of any SME. In the 1970s, laws were more favourable to employees. But now, from 2014 onwards, there are certain laws enacted by the government that are more favourable to management. Therefore, management can take the decisions which are more beneficial to the company and not to the employees.

Conclusions

Though under MRTU and PULP Act 1971, certain labour laws are favourable to the employee side, but if the leadership is divided between two different leaders, it may create unrest in the industry. Due to this, sometimes management may take undue benefits from different leaders. Hence employee benefits would not percolate to the employees due to quarrels between two unions.

Case Questions

1. What were the reasons for industrial unrest in the company?

2. Justify the dismissal of the trade union leader and the committee members?

3. What is the legal position regarding casual workers in recognition of trade unions?

2

Entrepreneurial Spirit and Ethics

The Two Pillars of an Enterprise—A Case Study on How India's Godrej Group Channelled the National Spirit at Home and Abroad

Learning Objectives

Many business houses, especially among the family managed businesses in India, have since their inception been pro-founders and supporters of the idea of business ethics as fundamental in a gradient of the organizational Vision and Mission, making the same as a way even for day-to-day business transactions for all employees including board members.

The entrepreneurial spirit is exalted mainly through adopting an ethical umbrella and as a guiding force. The Tatas, Birlas, Godrej, Walchands, Bajaj Group are a few of the names who are role models for furthering the Indian entrepreneurial spirit.

A detailed study of the journey so far of any of the above group of businesses would serve as an epitome of how a single-minded approach to managing business empires without compromising core values and beliefs in ethical practices has helped these empires to grow to global dimensions in spite of temptations for growth through compromising on core values.

Employees of such organizations help perpetuate the culture of business transactions even in their day-to-day lives outside the company premises have become social reformers insisting on ethical behaviour in societies around ensuring peace and tranquillity.

Indian Business Case Studies. Varsha Parab, Ramesh Mahadik, and Diksha Tripathi, Oxford University Press.
© ASM Group of Institutes, Pune, India 2022. DOI: 10.1093/oso/9780192869432.003.0002

Synopsis

In 1989, when the vestiges of the license raj era still wove reams of red tape around Indian businesses, a management trainee at Godrej GE Appliances', Faridabad, office faced a dilemma. An excise tax collector wanted a Diwali 'gift' delivered at his residence. 'Or else ...'

After discussions with his seniors, the trainee turned up at the official's house the next day with a gift-wrapped box. At the visitor's insistence, the official unwrapped it to find a pack of Godrej soaps in various fragrances. The unspoken but clear message: 'The Godrej group is committed to ethical business. Don't expect anything else from us'.

The anecdote, narrated by Ranganatha Thota, the management trainee at that time, sums up an idea that Gurcharan Das, former CEO of Procter & Gamble India, has articulated: 'while India secured political independence in 1947, it got economic independence only with the 1991 reforms'.

In many ways, the business history of the Godrej Group, which dates back to 1897, mirrors the Independence movement. The group's founder Ardeshir Godrej left India for Africa in 1889 to practise law. But unwilling to commit perjury to advance his career, he returned home, where the freedom movement was gathering pace, with the birth of the Indian National Congress in 1885.

Case Details

Upon returning to India, Ardeshir Godrej became an early proponent of the swadeshi idea of economic self-reliance. An early venture to manufacture medical equipment failed owing to British protectionism, but the indefatigable entrepreneur cast his eye on lowly locks. The lock business was in the control of British and American manufacturers, but Ardeshir found a flaw in their products: their springs, used to work the levers, often gave way. Borrowing money to set up a shed in Lalbaug in Mumbai in 1897, he began making Anchor locks, which didn't have springs. They were well received in the market.

From that, he went on to manufacture safes, again exposing a chink in the foreign-made safes, which rendered them unreliable. He patented the door frame, double-plate doors, and lock-case, and sold his safes at half the price of foreign brands. So successful was this business that even the Queen, while on a tour of India in 1912, availed of the services of a Godrej safe.

Ardeshir, who had a Renaissance spirit that was always looking for new realms to conquer, then began manufacturing soap with vegetable oil, out of consideration for Hindu sentiments that disfavoured the use of animal fat. His soaps soon secured celebrity endorsements from Rabindranath Tagore, Dr Annie Besant, and C. Rajagopalachari. Despite the heavily skewed business landscape that protected British business interests, Godrej products held their own against multinationals.

By the time he died in 1936, Ardeshir had expanded Godrej's businesses into new areas. That year, Godrej & Boyce and Godrej Soaps posted revenues of ₹12 lakhs and ₹6 lakhs, respectively.

Consolidation Phase

Ardeshir's younger brother Pirojsha, who succeeded him, focussed on consolidation rather than expansion into new areas. By Independence, the group's revenues had grown five times to ₹90 lakhs.

In 1948, the company secured permission to construct its first manufacturing plant on a large parcel of land that Pirojsha had acquired in Vikhroli (in current-day Mumbai). What it manufactured first was not locks or safes, but secure ballot boxes for independent India's first elections in 1952.

To showcase Indian prowess in manufacturing—the original 'Make in India' campaign!—Godrej diversified into making typewriters in 1953. Only four of the 1,800 components were imported; even these were soon being made at home. At the Congress session at Avadi, in Madras, Jawaharlal Nehru stooped over a Godrej typewriter to tip-tap a few words, signalling India's early success in industrialization. Pirojsha then ventured into making refrigerators; in 1958, the first Indian fridge came with a ₹1,885 tag.

Pirojsha got his three sons on board: Sohrabji to look into the overall marketing of Godrej products, Burjorji to look after soaps, and Naval to look into typewriters, refrigerators, and hi-tech electronics.

Going Global

The 1960s were a decade of two wars, a drought, and rampant inflation. In 1963, in the midst of that crisis, Burjorji's son Adi Godrej took over the soaps business, which then had a turnover of ₹2.43 crore.

This was the decade when the group gained a global footprint. After a couple of false starts, it secured a foothold in Malaysia and, later, Singapore. By the 1970s, exports to Western Europe picked up.

Pirojsha passed away in 1972; by then, the third generation of the Godrej family was in the saddle, with Naval's son Jamshyd heading the steel business, while Adi took Godrej soaps to new heights.

By 1975, the group's exports touched ₹22 crores. Inspired by Japanese processes, it introduced the Godrej Management System, to improve productivity and reduce inventories.

The dawn of the 1980s was marked by fierce competition with Hindustan Lever in the soaps segment. 'We needed big ideas to take on the competition and for the first time a male protagonist was used to promote a soap brand', recalls advertising incharge Sam Balsara, who handled the Cinthol account. The campaign in 1985 featured Vinod Khanna on horseback and, later, Imran Khan. Both proved phenomenal hits.

Post-1991 Phase

When the gale force of economic reforms came sweeping in 1991, Godrej was poised for take-off. In the 25 years since, the group has grown into a $4.5 billion (₹30,000 crores) conglomerate, with an impressive global footprint.

These 25 years have also seen the group experiment, unsuccessfully, with joint ventures with GE, P&G, Sara Lee, Pillsbury, and Hershey. And in 2008, when the global financial crisis dragged down economies, the group, now into its fourth-generation leadership under Adi's daughter Tanya Dubash, underwent a rebranding exercise to extend the brand appeal to young customers.

Looking ahead, the group plans to stick to its growth target of '10× in 10 years' growing both organically and through acquisitions. Industry analysts feel the group will deliver. 'They truly walk the talk', says Nilesh Shah, Managing Director, Kotak Mutual Fund.

It has been 119 years since Ardeshir, the low-profile Parsi gentleman, implanted the Godrej flag in the land that adopted his Guderz tribe (from which the family name derives) that fled from Iran. In this time, the Godrej Group has established itself not only as an entrepreneurial success but also as a business that runs on strong ethical foundations.

As Safe as Godrej

The group's product portfolio ranges from soaps to safety devices to aerospace manufacturing. When independent India's first general elections were to take place in 1951–1952, the government had to find a manufacturer for the ballot boxes. It zeroed in on Godrej & Boyce, which was by then already known for its high-quality locks and lockers. The company's factory in Vikhroli started operations in July 1951 and produced 15,000 ballot boxes a day to meet the order of 12 lakh boxes from 23 states. The cost per box was ₹5.

'With external locks proving expensive, Nathalal Panchal, a workman at Godrej, devised a unique locking system. It could only be opened by breaking a pre-impressed insignia and manipulating the locking lever through the aperture covered by the insignia', explains Vrunda Pathare, chief archivist at Godrej. One of these ballot boxes adorns the conglomerate's archives in suburban Vikhroli.

Back in 1947, Godrej was not only offering security solutions but also started manufacturing cupboards and soaps. 'Soap production was a result of the vow to use swadeshi products in pre-independent India. Sir Ardeshir Godrej came out with a washing soap bar in 1918 and toilet soap in 1920', says Pathare. The first vegetable-oil soap was named 'No. 2' while No. 1 came in 1922. This soap continues to be popular in India even today.

The Godrej group's history does not begin from the 20th century. It was in 1897 in a tiny shed in Mumbai's Lalbaugh area that Ardeshir Godrej came out with a high-security lock, branded as Anchor. This shed eventually became the shopfloor for churning out various products using metal sheets. Today, however, operations have shifted entirely to Vikhroli.

Godrej was also called upon to provide safes for the Queen of England when she visited India in 1905. Today, Godrej Security Solutions caters not only to domestic clients but also to exports to 45 countries. The group's manufacturing extends even to aerospace components.

Generations of Godrej employees have grown up and followed in the footsteps of their parents and grandparents in the company. Javed Khan, Head of Operations at Hubble (the group's collaborative workspace division), says his grandfather Sikander Khan worked for 35 years in the electricity department and his father Amir Khan spent close to four decades in the group's manufacturing division.

'After studying in the UK, I joined Godrej in 2010. I have worked in other companies too, but I find the working conditions the best here', he says. The group not only takes care of employees' housing, schooling, and medical needs but it also offers freedom to work and execute ideas, says Khan. 'There is a culture of promoting entrepreneurship within the organisation. My business idea has been sponsored by the group', he adds.

Somewhat similar is the story of Khushnuma Khambatta, associate general manager at Godrej Interio. Her father worked for over four decades in multiple roles, from marketing to manufacturing. He retired in 2014, while Khushnuma had joined the group in 2001. 'When I was a kid, my father bought home books on the group. I grew up seeing a company that had an Indian fabric and a global vision. It made me want to work for Godrej', she says.

After evolving from manufacturing to marketing, the Godrej group is now focussed on design and innovation. It is this continuous reinvention of the group that stands it in good stead to thrive in the coming centuries as well.

Case Questions

1. Do you think that times have changed for business management to be a bit more relaxed on core values to avoid being excluded from opportunities for growth and profitability in global business?

2. The impact of automation and AI calls for higher skill levels and reducing employment opportunities for the bottom of the pyramid and increasing unethical ways of earning lively hood and maintaining social harmony; what would you suggest as a way out to avoid such lopsided socially dangerous and risky consequences in the longer term of implementing modern technology in organizations?

3

The Generation and Technology Gap

A Case Study on the Impact of Generation Gap and the Technology on HR

Learning Objectives

Today more than any other period in our lifetimes, we experience classical divisions and separations in the acceptable behavioural norms between X, Y, and Z generations. There are obvious signs of reduced comfort levels in the interactions and transactions between individuals belonging to different generations. This is more pertinent when core values of understanding and mutual respect are vitiated and replaced by forceful tolerance of major distortions in interpersonal behaviours.

As students of management, it is essential to understand this paradigm shift and focus the learning on issues involved to mitigate the level of discomfort since each one of them will need to navigate through all cycles of existence.

Synopsis

As the dynamics of the workplace have changed with the evolution of technology, the change in generations has also impacted the organizational fabric. Organizations today comprise three distinct generations with different mindsets, aspirations, and ethos. Generation X (Gen X) consists of those born between 1961 and 1980, while generation Y (Gen Y) consists of millennials, that is, those born between 1981 and 1995. The youngest is the generation Z (Gen Z), comprising people born between 1996 and 2010. In India, millennials account for nearly half of the working-age population, whereas Gen Z has just made its entry.

Indian Business Case Studies. Varsha Parab, Ramesh Mahadik, and Diksha Tripathi, Oxford University Press.
© ASM Group of Institutes, Pune, India 2022. DOI: 10.1093/oso/9780192869432.003.0003

Why the Conflict?

The start-up ecosystem in India got a boost with millennials (Gen Y) taking risks to start businesses. Millennials can be called 'key doers', but they do need the wisdom and experience of the previous generation to help them scale up the business or execute the strategy to its full potential.

'Gen X and Y align valuable strategies in an organization. Their primary motivation is empowerment, and liberty to create something bigger along with wealth creation. Even the other two generations need empowerment but they will also need a lot of direction'.

Gen Z, who is entering the workforce, is the future of the businesses, which are being disrupted by digitalization all around. It is important to engage, encourage and listen to them; otherwise, the organization is likely to miss out on the disruption. And if that happens, it will become extinct.

The coexistence of all the three generations is critical for organizational success. Gen X is driven by passion, wealth, and achievements, while millennials are driven by work–life balance and quality of work. Gen Z, being multi-taskers, value independence more.

'Gen X aligns with valuable strategies in an organization. Their primary motivation is empowerment, liberty to create something bigger along with wealth creation. Even the other two generations need empowerment but they will also need a lot of direction'.

Being raised differently, the younger generation has views, outlooks, and perspectives that are in contrast to the previous generations. They are highly tech-enabled and prefer texting rather than talking. They are very inventive and innovative and enjoy challenging the status quo.

Millennials are the 'sandwich generation', stuck between both. They don't like to clock long hours at work and demand work–life balance, unlike the previous generation, which hoped for the same. It is because when Gen X started working, the economy and environment were tough, and hence, they got trained in a different way.

Where Is the Conflict?

Some thought leaders in the HR industry feel it's the skill gap and the psyche of the previous generations, which lead to interpersonal issues at the workplace. 'Nowadays, it's not about re skilling but rather about acquiring a new skill set altogether that creates a difference. The older generation is trapped in their own thinking that poses a challenge to learning new skill.' In view of fixed mindsets and beliefs.

For instance, in the manufacturing industry, someone who has spent relatively 10–15 years with one technology may suddenly become redundant. The previous experience can become a roadblock in the adoption of the new technology, which can lead to ego hassles. Today, employees get promoted much early and don't hold the same position for more than three years on average. The newer generation is expressive, liberal, demanding, and will not compromise easily with their expectations, which may also lead to confrontations. They are more open to discussing career issues and choices; they voice concerns; and look for a wider purpose in their actions.

The major disconnect occurs when seniors don't realize this and become rigid in their style. There has to be a realization that the style of management which worked 20 years back will not work now', 'Loyalty may not matter for newer generations, but the same cannot be confused with commitment—they are committed till they are with you'.

How to Coexist?

Every generation has its own set of problems and the previous generation has to be considerate about them. The issues arising out of multi-generation workforces become more evident and dysfunctional when one chooses to ignore. The best way to address issues is to connect with different stakeholders on a continuous basis, get a pulse, understand, and act on issues bothering them.

It is important to set the expectations of the generation right and moderate them. Each generation has a role to play for the next generation and the need to mentor, coach, and invest time to build the people and team, The leaders will fall short in time, and hence, Gen Y has to reciprocate the same support received from the previous generation to diffuse any conflicts at the workplace.

The issues arising out of multi-generation workforces become more evident and dysfunctional when one chooses to ignore. The best way to address issues is to connect with different stakeholders on a continuous basis, get a pulse, understand and act on issues bothering them'. To manage the generational differences, the organizations can create a positive culture and policies that are tuned to their demands.'

Flexibility is the key to managing people today, but at the same time, the manager has to clearly spell out the outcomes and deliverables. There is no harm in having an open discussion with the previous generation. They will need help to unlearn the previous skills and get equipped to adapt to new skills. The best way for organizations to deal with such a diverse workforce is to make them realize that they have to respect and provide space to each other.

There should be provisions to create 'life at work'. For instance, if employees have to work for 12–15 hours a day, the organization can intersperse these hours with fitness activities, such as yoga, gym, or coffee hours to socialize, so that these employees can live other aspects of their life. It is obvious that the demography of our workforce will move to include Gen Y and beyond. Organizations will no longer have a choice but to make the workplace congenial, which suits this shift.

HR–AI Conflict

The challenge for HR will be to understand how technology blends with the human workforce. It's a great time where AI and other technology frees us up from the administrative low-value jobs and allows talent to up-skill themselves. It is difficult to believe that machines will ever replace the creativity, imagination, and ideations that humans do. It will be a man and machine world where we use technology to add more value to our work and to the meaning of what we do.

How can technology improve the way HR approaches talent? What we are looking at is how we use AI and data to really understand our people. You get to really understand a talent as a wholesome person with the insights you can draw from AI and data. 'It's no longer about particular skills but what drives them, what's the psychometrics behind them. What really drives the productivity and the bottom line of any organization is known when you understand people that much better, and they will be more engaged and deliver a lot more'.

The insights AI can provide range from recruitment to development to team dynamics. If you don't understand your people, you will always see a conflict in the workplace. If you really go to the level of understanding human behaviours and why they do what they do, what is in their nature, characteristics, and life stories that shape them, it changes your perspective as well. It gives a lot more flavour to working relationships as well.

How Then Is HR Evolving as a Department amongst Industry 4.0?

HR teams need to get better at communicating their goals. When you talk about HR policies or practices, you can't speak from a language of governance or policing. You have to change the tone for the business to understand what is in it for them. It's about achieving that sweet spot between meeting employees' demands to the organization's ones. Sometimes when we make a policy or practice, it's really for the greater good but it's never communicated that way. The objective is to explain why we do this and what the end game in mind is. When that starts to happen, people will be much more accepting and understanding.

Now it's about humanizing HR because traditionally, it has always been from an administrative, governance, and policing approach and that is changing. We have to change; otherwise, we won't retain the best talent.

Another priority is people, more specifically, how we now change the mindset of people behaving in a different world. 'Our world is more agile therefore we have to be more empowered and enabled. We also can't have a one-size-fits-all approach to policies and practices. We can have a certain base but different aspects will need to change'.

The approach of HR has mostly been mechanical, for example, saying what's the policy we need to change and what's the system we need to change. Now we are flipping that and saying what the experience that we really want to create is? And that experience will then drive the philosophy, which will, in turn, drive the systems we want in place.

In regard to methodologies, the team has begun to adopt a 'Design Thinking' approach for HR transformation. The beauty of design thinking is it's really coming from looking through the customer's lens. The customers in the context of HR are the employees traditionally, it's been about solving HR's pain points, but the right approach should be about eliminating employees' pain points, or the business as a whole. By using design thinking, you approach the problems from a different lens and therefore get very different outcomes and solutions. It's the people solutions we need to solve.

Design thinking is about going into a deeper level of 'Critical Thinking' and finding the root cause. It can change HR itself because it's a completely new way of doing things. The benefit of a design thinking approach is that solution turnaround is quicker. With design thinking, the approach is sprint-led. It's an iterative process. There's also a behavioural change as it will not be perfect the first time around; look at start-ups for inspiration to implement design thinking. Want to know how they can churn things out really quickly? And they adopt design thinking, sprints, and iterative methodologies that could start changing the thinking itself.?

What have been the successes so far? Did we want to change the whole experience? What came out of our design sprints were a lot of solutions that were actually simple to adopt?

There were both quick wins and ones which will need a bit more time to implement. The other key area is filling and matching talent. 'We should build in-house algorithms to help with matching. Build prototypes for top talent and use it to see how one can scale it up for the organization'.

As HR teams look to radically transform to adapt to a new working culture, how will it evolve over the next few years? HR will become the advisory and consultant roles for the organization. A lot of the transactional jobs will be digitalized, which will free up HR to focus on higher-value work.

There will be a self-driven culture, not waiting for HR to tell you what training to go on but to be proactive on what you want to learn—leaving HR to fulfil the consultancy role. HR is one of the departments most affected by the generation gap, digitalization, as well as what technology and tools to implement; the question is how the very nature of HR teams will transform?

Case Questions

1. HR/Employee Relations (ER) as a function seem to have been caught into a vortex of multi-disciplinary changes in the demands

on its deliverables. The changes that are major in nature cannot be wished away both in terms of generation gaps and simultaneous technological outreaches. How do you think the organizations could afford an HR/ER activity, effectively managing the paradox?

2. The normal functions of recruitment/selection are being outsourced; what is left is talent/skill mapping; Learning and Development (L&D) to ensure talent retention/renewal is totally in alignment with and capable of meeting (at times crazy) market forces of poachers and ensuring employee loyalty. HR is becoming akin to the front desk job of a hotel trying to keep its customers employees happy and satisfied at all times. How could one make HR/ER job to be innovative and contributive, and enjoyable at the same time?

3. The present-day employee stress due to reasons beyond real job-related issues such as family discord, especially in case both husband and wife being employed, which is almost 100% in all cases, no time for family life entirely dependent on online food, congested, and compromised living conditions, stress due to liabilities of housing loan, car loans (EMI way of life), frustrating traffic jams, long distances, no one to call as relatives, disowned by societal/family gatherings feeling completely drained out each day as one heads home words.

Added to the above are fears of losing the job mainly due to falling short in the skill sets required. How can modern HR/ER iron out these distresses while themselves being a part of the system?

4

Building an Ethical and Smart Organization

Learning Objectives

All businesses are complex organizational systems that are nested within larger systems, such as national cultures and legal and regulatory systems, and composed of individuals who bring their own values and perspectives to work.

This interplay of personal, organizational and regulatory systems creates a dynamic environment that must be actively managed by leaders to promote the company's long-term success. Ethical failure at any level can bring catastrophe, but achieving good ethics at all levels yields enormous benefits in trust, efficiency and happiness.

Synopsis

In difficult financial times, companies face various moral issues to try to keep up with their competitors. Although these issues have a direct impact on employee decision making, businesses rarely address how employees should assess the ethics of their actions and incorporate ethics into their decisions. Often this can be alleviated by creating and maintaining a corporate culture with a focus on ethics. Corporate culture is often considered to be both a source of various problems and the basis for solutions and is certainly a factor that determines how people behave in an organization. The role of management in the organizational culture is important as it both acts as a role model for the employees and can also directly influence the behaviour and culture to improve

Indian Business Case Studies. Varsha Parab, Ramesh Mahadik, and Diksha Tripathi, Oxford University Press. © ASM Group of Institutes, Pune, India 2022. DOI: 10.1093/oso/9780192869432.003.0004

organizational performance. Of course, there are better methods that management can use to incorporate ethics into the corporate culture or increase the likelihood that its employees will act ethically and these methods are explored.

The Reality

When one evaluates the reasons for the fall of companies such as Enron, Lehman Brothers and WorldCom, what connects the dots is a stupefying disregard for ethics. Closer home, Ranbaxy's recent run- in with the US Food and Drug Administration has invited renewed questions about the governance, compliance and ethics practices of a section of firms in India and indeed across global economies.

While there is no reassurance in stating that incidents like Ranbaxy or Wockhardt or the fact that some of India's best- selling small cars have failed independent crash tests conducted by a global car safety watchdog are aberrations rather than reflections of a systemic problem, misconduct within its own walls remains one of the most lethal threats to any organization. Put in another way, a lack of ethics is like a missed opportunity in a world where competitive advantage is fast becoming a commodity. Says Rita McGrath, a professor at Columbia Business School, and author of The End of Competitive Advantage, "Companies can build advantages on the basis of ethics.

High ethical standards tend to be correlated with other positive attributes such as attention to quality, fair dealings with people and transparency that can give organizations an advantage." Needless to say, the benefits of good corporate governance and a culture of ethics percolate down to all levels of stakeholders —investors and top- quality employees are attracted to ethical companies.

Given that, what are the challenges that prevent companies from embracing and—more importantly—sustaining a culture of ethics and good conduct? What are the ways in which companies can ensure they don't stray from their intent at the time of establishment? And what is the best way to react if a situation involving an ethical transgression does arise?

Ethical Corporate Culture

In his book The Tipping Point, Malcolm Gladwell has spoken about the 'Broken Windows' theory that draws from the field of criminology. It states that crime tends to increase in situations where the atmosphere reflects that 'anything goes'. If a broken window is not repaired, it somehow gives a message that it is okay to break more windows. The norm applies in the corporate setting too.

Integrity, which is one of the core values of any organization, should be held above all other forms of behaviour. 'At the heart of an ethical culture are the shared values and assumptions of the people in the organization. These provide the overall direction for the behaviour of employees,' says Mona Cheriyan, Director, human resources, ASK Group.

'A strict enforcement of codes of compliance and a culture of zero intolerance for malpractices and frauds deter any probable ethical lapses,' adds AbhayGupte, senior director, Deloitte.

Having said that, it is difficult for a company to decide and craft an ethical corporate culture somewhere down its journey. It has to be done right at the beginning. 'It should be in the DNA of the promoters and leaders, and must be part of everything that the company does from day one,' says Narayan PS, vice-president and head, sustainability, Wipro.

While we know that senior leaders set the tone for action, they do not by themselves achieve the outcome for the organisation. It is how leaders act to promote right action that determines the performance and the culture. 'While ethical codes may vary from company to company, the basic fabric remains the same,' says Dilep Misra, president and head, corporate human resources, JK Tier.

At all times, management must take cognisance of staff turnover and grievances, customer complaints, product defects and returned items, expressed dissatisfaction of contractors and suppliers, cases of litigation triggered by unethical behaviour, and community unhappiness with corporate behaviour as reflected by media reports, citizen protests etc. 'The prevailing environment in society is so poor and corruption is so widespread, that creating an oasis of ethics is challenging. The only way out is that the tone has to be set at the top, else ethics will just be lip service,' says Ravi Venkatesan, author and former chairman, Microsoft India.

Ethics also includes placing the organization's interest before the promoter's interest. 'For instance, the employment of a promoter's son should be driven on merit and not on anything else,' says Harish Mariwala, chairman & MD, Marico.

Often those integrity failures are a result of senior individuals crossing ethical boundaries. 'In a hurry to reach to the top and to beat competition, they compromise on ethics,' says author and leadership guru Ms. Rao One must note that having a culture of ethics and compliance in a corporation is not a guarantee that there will not be breaches. What saves a company is the swiftness with which it redresses its wound.

Formal Elements of Ethical Culture

The Tata Group, known for its high 'trust' quotient, believes creating an ethical culture is a journey 'from compliance to commitment to consciousness'. 'It is not a question of the number of rules, but embedding desired values in each employee's consciousness, so that ethical conduct is a spontaneous output,' says Mukund Rajan, member, group executive council and chief ethics officer, Tata Sons.

To make core values explicit, and to demonstrate how they translate into behaviour in the daily business, an organization should establish formal norms, including codes of conduct, and guidelines and these should be led from the top, says Cheriyan of ASK Group.

Some prerequisites can help a corporation foster ethics in its DNA: there should be clearly enunciated policies, a basic code of conduct, regular communication with employees and a swift investigation system in case of reported malpractices. Here the perspective and role of corporate boards of directors in overseeing ethics and compliance matters within their firms cannot be underestimated.

The Board could also insist on a compliance certificate every quarter, and this certificate ought to be vetted by the audit committee. In fact, audits are good detection mechanisms to keep a tight leash on transgressions—a type of consequence management. In simple words, audits form the execution part of an ethical culture. While internal audits help create a culture of ethics, external audits give out a message to outsiders about the internal culture of ethics. 'The Board must mete out punishment, including sacking the CEO if he is found guilty,' says TV Mohandas Pai, chairman, Manipal

Global Education Services, and an ex-Infosys hand. 'Once the punishment is certain, the culture is firmed up.' That is the easier part, the benefits of which have been well documented. What is critical is to understand that ethics is different from compliance. The latter is the straightforward 'rules and regulations' part of ethics, and doesn't require high education. Ethics is a larger universe that goes beyond just following the law, and therefore, reflects how a company is oriented. It is possible for a company to be legally compliant and yet not have a strong culture of ethics.

The process of creating a culture of ethics probably starts from the process of recruitment. While hiring a person, it is not enough to assess only his/ her professional and technical competencies. It is equally important to look at the fit with the values of integrity and ethics. Here's how Wipro does it: its employees—campus and lateral hires—are inducted into Wipro's ethics journey at the very start of their association with the company. Thereafter, mandatory annual test and certification process, leadership training sessions, electronic mailers, posters etc constantly guide employees to follow the Wipro Code of Business Conduct (COBC). Any breach of COBC, identified from concerns raised through Wipro's Ombuds process, is handled swiftly and with seriousness, reveals Padmanabhan A, similar plane, the Board at JK Corporation meets every quarter to check on compliance breaches.

Challenges for Sustaining an Ethical Culture

But sustaining an ethical culture doesn't come without its challenges. It is particularly difficult to create and sustain this culture in a dispersed global organization. First, you have to define the culture and create a shared meaning of ethics across the organization. For instance, a media house may prohibit giving or receiving gifts, which could be an ethical guideline. But in India, gifting is accepted as part of culture, so a guideline like that could go against the popular wisdom, which poses a challenge.

Second, how do you propagate the non- negotiable? 'If you define many things under ethics, the education challenge in the company is high,' says Santrupt Misra, CEO, Carbon Black Business and group HR director, AdityaBirla Group. But the real moment of truth is how a company reacts to the ethical crisis. Does it wait for someone to point it out or accept it publicly and make corrections proactively? Or worse—does it play the blame game? That apart, ambitious Indian company wanting to play the global field must bear in mind that often, norms of the West may be more stringent than the ones back home. Critical lapses may not be overlooked so easily, as the case of Ranbaxy demonstrates. This is also a shift from the experiences of the past, when expectations from Indian companies were low. 'It is now important for corporate India to match up to global standards,' says Mariwala.

A handful of companies The Strategist spoke to argued if they were to comply with all the innumerable laws, it will slow processes down. 'But in the long run, look at the damage you will do to your own reputation and brand salience if you don't comply. You will have a longer ground to cover,' says Rajeev Dubey, president, group HR, corporate services and aftermarket, Mahindra & Mahindra. 'At the end of the day, good reputation means good business. And reputation can't be outsourced.'

SMART Ranbaxy's recent run- in with the US Food and Drug Administration has invited renewed questions about how to strengthen compliance mechanisms and ethical leadership within firms.

Conclusions

Ethical issues have posed major challenges to companies in recent years and there will undoubtedly be more in the future. Good ethical practices may not be easy to maintain. However, with a well-designed ethics policy, ethical leadership and implementing ethics into organizational strategies and processes, it will make it easier. The reason is because these factors are incorporated into the organizational culture.

How can a culture of character be developed? It is certainly by intention. It is the responsibility of particular individuals within the organization, i.e. Its leadership. Strong leaders model and pass on ethical aspects of the culture and use techniques like structure, decision-making processes, rewards, norms, heroes, stories, rituals and other artifacts to create a strong culture. This is the foundation for creating a culture of character, where members of the organization 'know what is right, value what is right, and do what is right.'

In all cases, management must be committed to ethical conduct. To conclude, despite the economic crisis, there are clear and long-lasting advantages of establishing an ethical culture. With a more open and ethical organizational culture, the more positively employees tend to commit to corporate social responsibility and this will generate more honest environments. As a consequence, this may not only reduce the unhealthy environment that began the financial crisis, but will also help in restoring the health of the financial system that caused it.

Case Questions

1. Are workers at all levels encouraged to take responsibility for the consequences of their behaviour? To question authority when they are asked to do something that they consider to be wrong? How?

2. What is your overall evaluation of the organizations ethical culture? What are its areas of strength and weakness?

3. Does a formal code of ethics and/ or values exist? Is it distributed? How widely is it used? Is it reinforced in other formal systems, such as reward and decision-making systems?

5

Succession Planning in Tata Group

A Case Study on the Difficulties Faced by Tata Group Companies

Learning Objectives

The major groups of industries like the Tata Group are considered as role models of excellence in implementing corporate governance norms as also as organizations which initiated social reform activities even before the regulatory authorities took note of the necessities of such corporate responsibilities.

However, over the previous 8–10 years, incidences and events happening at even at board level in organizations such as Tatas and Infosys, the two at pole positions for others to follow, indicate major slips in the understanding of Corporate Governance (CG) norms and other norms of interactions.

The drawn-out board room battles and the public spillover of lack of mutual respect and disbeliefs leading to extended Courtroom litigations are compelling students of management and even industry executives to sit up and take note of such incidences while learning relevant aspects in business ethics and corporate governance subjects.

Synopsis

This case study is suitable to introduce the concept of Succession planning and its significance. Succession planning is a process for identifying and developing new leaders, who can replace old leaders when they leave, retire or die.

Indian Business Case Studies. Varsha Parab, Ramesh Mahadik, and Diksha Tripathi, Oxford University Press.
© ASM Group of Institutes, Pune, India 2022. DOI: 10.1093/oso/9780192869432.003.0005

History shows the need for proper succession planning as many companies opted with comeback of their renowned leader. Back in 1997, Apple brought back founder Steve Jobs when the company was in trouble. Howard Shultz, who left Starbucks in 1986 to start his own chain of espresso bars, was back not once but twice. Narayana Murthy was back at Infosys when things were not rosy with the IT bellwether. Ratan Tata handed over the baton to Cyrus Mistry and returned back four years later in 2016.

This case study discusses the succession planning of Tata GROUP after the retirement of Ratan Tata in the year 2012 and his comeback in the year 2016.

Case Details

History shows the comeback of renowned leader's need of many top fortune companies. Many of them rose because of improper handover of position. The process of identifying and developing new leaders is known as succession planning.

What Is Succession Planning?

Succession planning can be defined as purposeful and systematic efforts made by an organization to ensure leadership continuity, retain and develop knowledge and intellectual capital for the future and encourage individual employee growth and development (Schein 1997: cited in Caruso, Gorehler & Perry, 2005).

Objectives of Succession Planning

(1) To identify and plan for critical work positions, by developing a pool of potential successors and encouraging a culture that supports knowledge transfer and employee development.

(2) To build human resource programs that attract and retain qualified individuals.

(3) To implement a framework that identifies the competency requirements of critical positions, assesses potential candidates,

and develops required competencies through planned learning and development initiatives.

Challenges in Succession Planning

(1) Lack of funding for leadership development
(2) Inability to locate or create a pool of active and passive candidate
(3) Lack of assessment tools
(4) Lack of succession planning tools and career development tools
(5) Inability to identify the future talent needs of the organization f) Lack of interest from senior executives

Guiding Principles

(1) Supports the five fundamental values of the New Brunswick public service: integrity, respect, impartiality, service, and competence.
(2) Conducted in accordance with the Civil Service Act, its regulations and the policies established by the board of management.
(3) Strikes a balance between the values of fairness, accessibility, transparency, and efficient use of government resources for current and future needs.
(4) Aligned with current and future business needs of government and departmental/agency strategic plans.
(5) Aligned with the goals of the corporate HR plan and the executive development strategy to develop current and aspiring leaders.
(6) Candidates are assessed using methods that are competency-based and free from favouritism.
(7) Communication is open and transparent.

Benefits of Succession Planning

(1) Aligning strategic goals and human resources to enable the 'right people in the right place at the right time' to achieve desired business results.

(2) The development of qualified pools of candidates ready to fill critical or key positio

(3) Providing stability in leadership and other critical positions to sustain a high-performing public service and ensure the uninterrupted delivery of services and programs.

(4) Identifying workforce renewal needs as a means of targeting necessary employee training and development.

(5) Helping individuals realize their career plans and aspirations within the organization.

(6) Improving employees' ability to respond to changing environmental demands.

(7) The opportunity for timely corporate knowledge transfer succession planning process.

Introduction of Tata Group

Tata Group is an Indian multinational conglomerate holding company. It was founded in 1868 by Jamsetji Tata, headquartered in Mumbai, Maharashtra, India. It gained international recognition after purchasing several global companies. It is owned by 'Tata Sons'. Tata Sons is the promoter of the major operating Tata companies and holds significant shareholdings in these companies.

There are 29 publicly listed Tata enterprises with a combined market capitalization of about $145 billion as of November 2017. Tata companies with significant scale include Tata Steel, Tata Motors (Jaguar, Land Rover), Tata Consultancy Services, Tata Power, Tata Chemicals, Tata Global Beverages, Tata Teleservices, Titan, Tata Communications, and Indian Hotels (Taj Hotels). The board of directors and shareholders of Tata Group guide and supervise each Tata company or enterprise independently.

Tata companies are commonly referred to as the Tata group and the Chairman of Tata Sons as chairman of the Tata group. The company's principal activities are:

i   To invest in operating companies to support their growth
ii   To promote and invest in new businesses
iii To maintain its shareholding in major operating companies

Journey of Ratan Tata from Apprentice to Chairman

In the case of Ratan Tata, he was a surprise choice to head the group after JRD. He joined as an apprentice on the shop floor of its Jamshedpur plant in 1962. In 1971, he was appointed director-in-charge of the ailing National Radio and Electronics Co. While Tata managed to turn around the firm's fortunes, it was to be a temporary success. In 1977, he was asked to turn around another troubled company, the Mumbai-based Empress Mills. Tata managed to do so. He became chairman in 1991, almost after 30 years. By then, he knew the group inside out.

In 2002, when Ratan Tata was set to retire at 65, the Tata Sons board re-designated him as non-executive chairman so that he could continue for another five years.

In 2005, the board increased the retirement age of non-executive directors to 75, ensuring that Tata would be in office till 2012. And finally, when he packed his bags at Bombay House and handed over the baton to Cyrus Mistry, it was only to return four years later in 2016.

Previous Pattern of CEO

Some see a pattern and attribute it to Ratan Tata's push to lower the average age of senior management in the group. N. Chandrasekaran was handpicked to take over as CEO of tech giant Tata Consultancy Services at 46 in 2009. R. Mukundan took the reins of Tata Chemicals at 42 in 2008, the same year Brotin Banerjee became CEO of Tata Housing at 35 and Mukund Rajan, then 40, was appointed head of Tata Teleservices (Maharashtra). N. Srinath got the top job at Tata Communications in 2007 when he was 45.

The Race for Succession

Tata Sons, the holding company of the Tata Group, announced the members of the five members Committee announced to find a successor to the Group Chairman Ratan Tata who is due for retirement by December 2012.

The Selection Committee Members Include

(1) N. A. Soonawala, vice-chairman of Tata Sons.
(2) Shirin Bharucha, a lawyer who has worked with Tata Group for several years.
(3) R. K. Krishnakumar, director, Tata Sons.
(4) Cyrus Mistry, board member, Tata Sons and an outsider.
(5) Lord Bhattacharya, Director WMG-Innovative Solutions.

The search committee has now gone beyond the brief of merely searching for a leader and recommended a restructuring of the Tata Sons board by bringing in independent directors and younger executives from group companies. The search for a successor was done for almost one year after the committee being formed. Executives nominated for becoming successor (by committee):

Challenges for Committee for the Selection of Successor

(1) Looking for someone to run Tata Sons (which is a holding company) or someone to head the whole group, which is what Ratan Tata is doing now?
(2) Why a professional CEO with the experience of running multinational companies should join a group's privately owned holding company? As in Ratan Tata's case, the jobs of Tata Sons' chairman and group executive head were combined. And he was a Tata. The same symbolized the unity of the two objectives—being head of the holding company and boss of the group.
(3) Can a non-Tata manage to do both?

To answer this, we need to understand the business of Tata Sons. It is a holding company, and its main business is to get its shareholdings to deliver returns. In short, its business is portfolio management. The purpose of hiring a professional CEO is to maximize shareholder value. A holding company needs a fund manager and not just a professional CEO. Is it any surprise Indira Nooyi, Arun Sarin, and others have not expressed any great enthusiasm for a fund management job? Hence resulting in selecting Cyrus Mistry.

Reasons for Choosing Cyrus Mistry

(1) A major shareholder in Tata Sons.
(2) A graduate in civil engineering from Imperial College, London.
(3) Already on the board of Tata Sons from August 2006 and proved *his* quality and calibre from his participation, his astute observations, and his humility.
(4) Experience of being a managing director in Shapoorji Pallonji Mistry's Construction Group.
(5) Age and belonging to Parsi religion.
(6) His career achievements and his financial knowledge were considered at the time of his vote.
(7) The family is very familiar with the Tatas and that could be one of the influencing factors and the only person who knows totally about Tata than compared to other people shortlisted for the post.

Succession Process

Cyrus Mistry joined Tata Sons as a board member in August 2006.

After his selection as a successor of Mr. Ratan Tata in 2011, he had been appointed as a deputy chairman of Tata Sons. Ratan Tata worked with Cyrus Mistry for a year to give him the exposure, the involvement, and the operating experience to equip him to undertake the full responsibility of the group after his retirement.

Welspun Acquisition

The latest trigger was Tata Power's acquisition of Welspun Renewables' solar and power assets—the deal went through without consultation with the Tata Sons board.

Management Restructure

The 48 year old has been trying to shake up the $100 billion company by changing the management structure to bring in new faces at senior levels. He has also battled issues on a number of, including a costly settlement with Japanese telecom operator NTT Docomo and the sale of Tata Steel's loss-making UK business. Britain's vote in June to exit the European Union was a big setback for the steel sale, which Tata has now put on hold.

Brexit has also cast a shadow over Tata Motors' luxury car unit Jaguar Land Rover (JLR), which has a large UK manufacturing base. Tata Motors' quarterly profit halved as the pound slumped following the Brexit vote, and JLR's CEO warned that some customers in Europe, its biggest market, no longer wanted to buy British cars.

Case Questions

1. What are the possible reasons for the failure of succession planning in the above case?

2. What are the pitfalls for succession planning?

3. What factors need to be considered while training the successor at the CEO level?

4. Whether one year time period is sufficient for complete hand over of big company like Tata Group.

SECTION II

CASE STUDIES IN FINANCE MANAGEMENT

*Direct/Indirect Taxation, Banking, and Insurance
are All Areas of Financial Accounting*

6

A Case Study in Private Equity and Venture Capital Funds

Learning Objectives

The case is drafted keeping in mind students of postgraduate, undergraduate, and industry professionals with specialization in finance who have a keen interest in capital market, its growth, and risk associated in the capital market.

Classical business cycle and management ideas learned from masters such as Schumpiter, Karl Mark, and M. Kayens help students comprehend how important investment decisions are made in relation to company cycles and likely prospects.

Major fund firms, on the other hand, are routinely observed investing in ways that are counter to cyclical investment theories and risk avoidance notions. Rather than prescribed procedures, this counter-cyclical investment strategy is frequently based on hunches and gut reactions.

This case study attempts to take students on a trip of counter-cyclical investment decisions made by big venture capitalists and stockbrokers on a regular basis, explaining the psychology and practice used in such investments.

Synopsis

Vultures are frequently used as a disparaging term to characterize how some private equity (PE) funds operate. However, a few PE funds that dared to invest between 2011 and early 2014years—when India's economic development slowed dramatically—can be compared favourably to birds of prey.

Indian Business Case Studies. Varsha Parab, Ramesh Mahadik, and Diksha Tripathi, Oxford University Press.
© ASM Group of Institutes, Pune, India 2022. DOI: 10.1093/oso/9780192869432.003.0006

In 208 deals, two PE funds (IFC and Baring Private Equity) and four venture capital (VC) funds (Norwest Venture Partners, Sequoia Capital, Accel Partners, and Helion Venture Partners) spent around Rs 24,000 crore ($3.94 billion). In the three downturn years, this accounted for 13.4% of all PE and VC investments. Everyone, including PE funds, struggled during these years. According to Price Waterhouse Coopers, their investments decreased by $1 billion to $9.6 billion in calendar 2013. Between 2011 and 2013, the number of PE and VC deals fell by 17% to 418, with VC funds faring better than PE funds. These years were among the most challenging to do business in because of economic and political uncertainties, unfavourable currency volatility, domestic policy inertia, high inflation, and high cost of capital.

PE funds had to cope with scams and flameouts, as well as far too many instances of promoter-investor strife, in the midst of all of this. Due to the lack of liquidity in the financial markets, exiting investments has been difficult. The market was at an all-time low in terms of valuation. This was cited by the majority of PE funds as a reason to avoid investing. However, a few investors saw it as an opportunity to buy low and sell high. Only time will tell, but funds that took the latter approach are likely to be the fall's biggest winners.

The Case Details

'In any investment cycle, there will be downturns,' says Rahul Khanna, managing director of Canaan Partners. 'Funds look for companies that can withstand ups and downs.' Mayank Rastogi, partner, EY India, adds: 'In uncertain times, counter-cyclical methods can and have succeeded in the past for investors with deep sector expertise and comparatively longer investment horizons.'

Two funds stood out in the PE area. Baring Private Equity invested $1.05 billion in 15 acquisitions (including investments by Baring Asia Fund in India). International Finance Corporation's (IFC) private equity arm closed 33 deals for $910 million. According to data from business consultant firm Grant Thornton India, Tata Capital, the third most active fund in these three years, invested $274 million. Norwest Venture Partners, Sequoia Capital, and Accel Partners all spent about $600 million in the venture capital market. A total of $284 million was invested by Helion Venture Partners.

' "If you investigate deeply in a few industries, you have a good chance of catching a new trend," Rastogi continues. Good ideas/teams/companies can be distilled from a vast universe by such funds.'

Given the generally gloomy economic and market conditions throughout these three years, most of the deals made by these funds would have been at bargain prices. If GDP growth returns to above 7% and valuations rise over the next five years, funds that invested during the downturn could be the largest winners. There is sufficient data to suggest that funds taking a chance on a downturn can make a fortune.

Chrys Capital made a technology risk, buying 4% of HCL Technologies for $180 million in 2008, shortly after Lehman Brothers went bankrupt. Half of that was sold in January for $500 million. More exits will occur, although at a slower pace, now that stock markets are bouncing back. 'Sentimentally, the market is prepared for an uptick in PE transactions,' says Raja Lahiri, partner at Grant Thornton India. 'However, given the overhang of exit issues and the growth downturn in recent years, it's also too much to anticipate something spectacular to happen all of a sudden.'

Few dared to follow the countercyclical strategy were:

IFC

Financial Institutions Group (FIG), the PE investment arm of the IFC, made 33 investments totalling $910 million between 2011 and early 2014. This is consistent with its countercyclical investing philosophy. Inderbir Singh Dhingra, IFC equity head Asia Pacific, FIG, adds, 'We are countercyclical.' 'When others are afraid of taking chances, we come in.' IFC invested in unexpected enterprises like Cholamandalam Investment and Finance and Bandhan Financial Services, not only at an unlikely point in the economic cycle. Cholamandalam's personal loan business was in peril when IFC invested at the height of the financial crisis. 'It was a good company that was briefly hampered by a difficult external climate,' Dhingra explains. At an average price of '97 per share, IFC bought 8.26% of Cholamandalam'.

IFC invested 8.26% in Cholamandalam in December 2011 at an average price of Rs 97 per share and sold one-fourth in January 2014 at Rs 287 per share, nearly tripling its investment.

In 2011, IFC ventured on Bandhan, a microfinance firm, picking up 11% for $29.35 million, not just in the middle of the financial crisis, but also when the microfinance sector was in the news. 'We had a player that was relatively unscathed by the microfinance crisis, had good management, and was geographically diverse,' Dhingra says. In March, Bandhan was granted a banking licence, confirming IFC's belief in the company. 'A banking licence will lower Bandhan's cost of capital and provide significant value to its investors,' says Manoj Sharma, director of MicroSave, a microfinance consulting firm. 'Because it works with poor communities, Bandhan will play a vital role in financial inclusion.' IFC has 200 analysts on the ground who assess prospects and provide recommendations and investments.

Fortis Healthcare, Fino, Ratnakar Bank, and Parag Milk Foods are among the companies in which IFC has invested in recent years. It believes that being countercyclical means not only looking for bargains but also supporting the private sector. 'We don't believe in maximising profits in a short period of time.' 'Money is important, but it isn't enough,' Dhingra concludes. 'We also consider the goal of development.' The IFC invests $300–500 million in India every year. Deals since 2011–33* (*including Bandhan Financial Services, Fino, and Parag Milk Foods), total deals—50+ value of deals since 2011—$910m.

Norwest Venture

In its first five years after entering India in 2006, Norwest made only a dozen investments. In the next three years, when the economy slowed down appreciably, it struck almost two dozen deals, pumping in $598 million. This is more than any VC fund in India, though Norwest also made some investments outside the pure-play VC space. 'Norwest has been a prolific investor,' says a venture practice head of a large audit and consultancy firm. Norwest has invested in an odd mix of emerging internet businesses and old-world listed companies.

Norwest made barely a dozen investments in the first five years after entering India in 2006. It signed roughly two dozen deals for $598 million over the next three years, when the economy slowed significantly. Norwest made more investments outside of the pure-play VC industry than any other VC firm in India. A venture practice leader at a prominent audit and consulting firm notes, 'Norwest has been a prolific investor.' Norwest has made investments in a strange combination of new online start-ups and established public enterprises.

Quikr, Yatra, PepperFry (furniture seller), FashionAndYou (fashion web store), and Capillary Technologies are among the portfolio firms in the first category (provider of research tools for online companies). 'Despite the uncertain circumstances, an ecosystem for venture-funded enterprises has been built in the last several years,' says Sohil Chand, managing director of Norwest India. 'Companies like Flipkart and In Mobi have sprung up as a result of this.'

It has invested in Cholamandalam Investment and Finance and Shriram City Union Finance in the old economy (which it exited early this year).

Norwest's India exposure is unusually large for a new fund. Because it only works in three countries: the United States, Israel, and India, this is largely to blame. 'Venture capital funds operate in four to five nations,' according to a rival fund's managing director, who asked to remain anonymous. 'Norwest invests its entire worldwide fund in only three markets, with India being the lone emerging market. As a result, a significant portion of its capital is concentrated in this region.'

Exits are now easier, according to the business, because stock markets are rallying—the Sensex has been up 22% this year. 'We will see companies go public to generate capital and unleash value,' Chand adds, without elaborating on Norwest's portfolio investment intentions. Thyrocare Technologies, a diagnostic services company with a market capitalization of Rs 1,500 crore, is considering going public in 2015–16. According to Grant Thornton, Norwest bought a 10% stake in Thyrocare in 2012 for $21.8 million.

Norwest exited Shriram City Union Finance in May, after a five-year return of four-fold. Persistent Systems and InMobi were both acquired by it in 2012 and 2011, respectively. So far, it's returned two to four times its initial investment. On the back of improving market sentiment, Chand expects higher returns presently. Risks exist as well. 'Our average invest-ments were made when the rupee was trading at less than 60 to the dollar,' Chand explains. 'As the local currency weakens, we're losing money.'

Deals since 2011–23* (*including Quikr, Komli Media, FashionAndYou, and PepperFry), value of deals since 2011—$598m, exits: Persistent Systems, Shriram Finance, and InMobi; returns 2X to 4X

Baring Private Equity Partners India

Despite making more investments than any other PE fund in the last three years, Baring India has avoided internet and e-commerce firms. RMZ Corp, Sintex, Shilpa Medicare, and Vardhaman Textiles, for example, are infrastructure, retail, real estate, manufacturing, and pharma enter-prises. It's not like it didn't look on the internet and in the e-commerce world. 'Our margin assumptions were significantly more aggressive than they turned out to be,' says Baring India managing partner Rahul Bhasin. 'Every company in which we lost money has underperformed our ex-pectations.' 'I don't have any regrets.'

Baring Asia Fund, a sibling fund, bought a 70% share in Hexaware Technologies in late 2013 and also owns Lafarge India, a cement com-pany. 'Both (Baring Asia and Baring India) have been there for a while,' says the head of a large audit and consulting firm's venture business. 'While the India fund has made a number of investments, the Asia fund has made the larger deals.' The one thing Baring regrets is the currency: it made a lot of investments when the dollar was in the Rs 45–47 range, and now it's around Rs 60. 'We've overcome that loss and gained some money,' Bhasin says, 'but it might be better.' Shilpa Medicare, for example, was trading at Rs 340 when Baring invested Rs 70 crore in it in early 2011. Although it reached a high of Rs 502 on July 8—a gain of 43%—rupee devaluation reduced the gain to just 10%. 'Government bonds pay out be-tween 8.5 and 9% annually. On top of that, we're looking at an 8% equity premium,' Bhasin adds.

Baring typically considers an investment horizon of 8–10 years. Bhasin believes that the broader macroeconomic situation has improved, making exits easier. 'Intentions to lower the fiscal deficit will reduce cur-rency pressure,' he argues. Is it worth taking the risk of investing in India during the slowdown? 'It hasn't totally paid off. Though things are looking up now,' Bhasin adds.

The BAF tale is as follows: Total deals: 40+, deals since 2011: 12 (including Shilpa, RMZ, Sintex, Redington, and TD Power), value of deals since 2011: $1,049 million (including Baring Asia investments in India), exits so far: BFL Software, SlashSupport, Jyothy Laboratories, and Mphasis.

Helion Venture Partners

Economic cycles don't seem to bother Helion. It is based on venture investing facts: one-third of investments fail, one-third return the money invested, and the rest are stars that return 5–15 times the money invested. Helion has made about 50 investments in India since it began in 2006. Taxiforsure.com, Today's Healthcare, and Vienova Education are among the 29 that have come since 2011.

Matrix Partners made 21 investments during the downturn, Norwest made 23, and Accel made 43 during the same time period, according to Grant Thornton. More than half of Helion's portfolio is made up of internet businesses. Yepme.com (a men's fashion e-tailer), babyoye.com (a baby product vendor), and taxiforsure.com are just a few of them (aggregator of cabs for rent). 'Helion targets specific industries, like as technology and the internet,' says the head of a renowned consultancy's PE practice. 'This helps in two ways: it makes it easier to see a new trend, and it allows them to sift through big portfolios for good companies.' The time it takes to grow up an internet firm is shortening, according to Sanjeev Aggarwal, senior managing director of Helion Venture Partners. 'We have a 7–10 year time horizon for leaving,' he says. 'As domestic spending rises, we anticipate easier exits.'

Helion has two options: locate a strategic investor (like RedBus and Letsbuy.com) or go public (Makemytrip.com). Aggarwal, on the other hand, sees certain obstacles. 'Technology is related to venture-backed enterprises, and technology skill is in real short supply,' he argues. 'Aside from that, there is a lack of regulatory certainty, which is out of a company's control.' To be 'excitable', according to Aggarwal, a company must be valued at $100 million. 'After that, they start tossing money around and gain in value.' Companies that aren't that big won't be able to attract big money from around the world.'

Total deals: 50; deals since 2011: 29* (*including Taxiforsure.com, Today's Healthcare, and Vienova Education); value of deals since 2011: $284 million; exits: RedBus, Make My Trip, Amba, and letsbuy.com.

Sequoia Capital

According to the account, while passing through Madhya Pradesh, a group of Sequoia Capital fund managers heard a radio jingle that piqued their interest. The tune advertised Indore-based Prakash Snacks' 'Yellow Diamond' potato chips. Sequoia invested $30 million in this local food manufacturer in 2011 after a few cold calls and six months. During the downturn years, Sequoia was on the lookout for such chances.

Vini Cosmetics, a deodorant manufacturer based in Ahmedabad, drew their notice in 2013. For Rs 100 crore, Sequoia purchased 9% of Vini. Vini's Fogg is now one of the top ten deodorant brands in a crowded market of 60, challenging multinationals like Hindustan Unilever. Sequoia has declined to be interviewed for this article. 'There may be some pessimism in government-driven sectors due to macroeconomic difficulties,' managing director VT Bhardwaj told ET at the time of the Prakash Snacks acquisition. Local food brands, on the other hand, represent a significant investment opportunity, with snacks being the fastest-growing category.' 'Sequoia completed 48 investments totalling $589 million between 2011 and Q1 2014, spanning industries such as internet, retail, finance, consumer, education, and biotech. 'Unlike most investors, Sequoia searches for opportunities in tier-II and tier-III cities as well,' says the PE practice head of a prominent audit and consulting firm who did not want to be identified. 'They're very research-oriented, productive, and have a keen sense of what's going on in the world.'

Case Questions

1. What are the key characteristics of a fund manager's counter-cyclical investment strategy—what are the business factors that allow these firms to take a risky approach to investment strategies?

2. How might recent initiatives outlined in the Indian government's annual budget affect the level of trust in these systems?

3. How can retail investors in these PE and VC funds evaluate their investment returns in light of the fund managers' high-risk activities?

7

Direct Taxation

Case Study on Retrospective Tax Laws—M/S Shell India and Shell Gas Bv

Learning Objectives

The impact of direct taxation laws enacted by the government from time to time is subject to periodical scrutiny by the tax authorities to keep a watch on tax evasion by major financial transactions, especially during share transfer actions by corporate companies having global partners as principal stakeholders in businesses.

There have major tax claims with penalty for attempted tax evasion by the concerned business leading drawn-out court battles both in domestic and international courts of law.

While on one hand, the Indian government has strong intentions and formulated regulations attracting huge direct investments from abroad, the tax authorities are catching up with collusions to exploit the loopholes in the existing provisions of financial transactions and tax payable thereon.

This case study highlights one of such conflicts between the tax authorities and the incumbent company Shell India a subsidiary of the Royal Dutch Shell group.

Synopsis

The transfer pricing has a significant role to play in terms of taxation of income from intangibles in case of intercompany transfer pricing in today's world.

Indian Business Case Studies. Varsha Parab, Ramesh Mahadik, and Diksha Tripathi, Oxford University Press.
© ASM Group of Institutes, Pune, India 2022. DOI: 10.1093/oso/9780192869432.003.0007

With special reference to the Shell case which is a wholly owned subsidiary of The Royal Dutch Shell Group, the amalgamation of two rival companies: Royal Dutch Petroleum Company and the 'Shell' Transport and Trading Company Ltd of the United Kingdom.

The Royal Dutch Shell Group was created in February 1907 through the amalgamation of two rival companies: Royal Dutch Petroleum Company and the 'Shell' Transport and Trading Company Ltd of the United Kingdom.

Case Details

Shell India Markets Pvt Ltd (Shell India) is a wholly owned subsidiary of the Royal Dutch Shell Group of Companies. Shell India Markets Private Limited (the taxpayer) had issued equity shares to its non-resident associated enterprises (AEs) at face value.

The Transfer Pricing Officer (TPO) alleged short receipt of consideration for the issue of shares and made an adjustment for the difference between the arm's length price (ALP) consideration (as computed by the TPO) and the consideration based on face value (as had been received by the taxpayer). The TPO also added an interest amount on the short receipt.

Aggrieved, the taxpayer filed a writ petition before the High Court of Bombay (HC) on the issue of jurisdiction, i.e., the jurisdiction of revenue to bring to tax amount received on capital account, viz., issue of equity shares to its AEs under Chapter X of the Indian Income-tax Act, 1961 (the Act).

Shell India had issued 870 million shares to Shell Gas BV in 2009 March, at Rs. 10 a share. However, the income tax department was of the view that the shares were grossly undervalued, and it valued them at Rs. 180 a share. Thus, the department added the difference to the taxable income of Shell India. Furthermore, the income tax department had issued a show-cause notice adding another Rs. 3,100 crore to Shell India's income for 2008–2009 in another transfer pricing case.

Being aggrieved, the company moved the Bombay High Court, challenging the tax notice. The tax authorities argued that the deal is a transfer pricing arrangement by which the share issued are undervalued and hence the company is liable to pay tax on the income generated out of it. The tax authorities also asked for tax on the interest the Anglo-Dutch Oil Company would have earned in cases of underpriced transfer of shares.

On the contrary, Shell Plc argued that the foreign parent's equity infusion into its subsidiary is not liable to be taxed, the same being Foreign Direct Investment which cannot be taxed. Shell Plc also denied the argument of the tax authority saying that the price of the share was perfectly valued and not undervalued.

The bench of Justices Bombay High Court decided on a petition filed by Shell India Markets. The court ruled in the favour of Shell Plc on the ground that, under the provisions of transfer pricing, the issuance of shares by an Indian Company to its foreign partner is **not taxable.** The judgment has specified that transfer-pricing laws cannot be imposed on shares issued to a foreign parent. It has been the practice of multinationals to fund their subsidiary by issuing shares, the court viewed it as a capital transaction thus not covered under the rule of transfer pricing.

The HC held that the jurisdiction to apply Chapter X of the Act would be occasion only when income arises out of an international transaction and such income is chargeable to tax under the Act.

Further, the HC held that the fact that the taxpayer chose not to declare the issue of shares to its AEs in Form 3CEB as in its understanding it fell outside the scope of Chapter X of the Act, now stands vindicated by the decision of the HC in the case of Vodafone India Services Private Limited. Moreover, the HC clarified that mere non-filing of Form 3CEB on the part of the taxpayer, would not give jurisdiction to levy tax an amount which is not liable to any tax in India if it is incorporated a company by the name Shell India Markets Pvt Ltd. as an Indian company.

To intensify its business proceedings in India, Shell India came out with the issue of equity shares in the year 2009. And the stage was well set for the IT Dept. to make its entry when all of such shares were bought by Shell Gas BV (Foreign Co.), i.e. nothing but Foreign (In)Direct Investment of Rs. 87 crores, the area of conflict being that all such shares were issued at Rs. 10 per share (18 US cents).

And here comes the twist in the story, the entry was late but it was the ultimate and latest thing that happened when IT Dept. sent a notice in January 2013 to Shell Gas BV depicting that Shell India was undervalued in connection with the equity issue in the March 2009 through which the shares issued to Shell Gas BV at Rs.10 per share, but the income-tax authorities peg the deal at Rs.183/share. It would challenge a tax departments' notice which claims that it underpriced a sale of shares to an overseas group company by $2.7 billion.

Protagonist

Contentions of Petitioner

The taxpayer contended that as per Section 92(1) of the Act: Prerequisite for application of this section is that the income should arise from an international transaction. In this case, no income arises from issue of equity shares and capital receipts are not income under the Act unless specifically provided for (Section 2(24) (xvi) of the Act).

(3) The taxpayer also upheld its view that the order of the TPO/DRP demonstrates that shortfall in premium on issue of shares is not taxable in as much as amount received by the petitioner on account of share premium has not been taxed. If there is any impact of income on account of business restructuring / reorganizing, then only such income would be subjected to tax as and when it arises, whether in present or in future. In this case, such a contingency does not arise as there is no impact on income which would be chargeable to tax due to issue of shares (Section 92B of the Act).

Section 92(2) of the Act: The objective is to ensure that profits are not understated nor losses overstated by disclosing higher cost or expenditure, than the benefit received. Hence it has no application in the present case.

(6) The view taken by revenue that if the petitioner had got the extra premium, he would have invested it somewhere and would have earned additional income is based on pure guesswork and is not admissible.

Contentions of Revenue Department

Section 92(1) of the Act: Uses the word 'Any income arising from an International Transaction'. This indicates that the income of either party to the transaction could be subject matter of tax and not the income of resident only. Under Chapter X of the Act, real income concept has no application; otherwise, the words would have been 'actual Income'. Section 2(24) of the Act: Income as defined is inclusive definition and it does not prohibit taxing capital receipts as income.

Section 2(47) of the Act: The issue of shares is a transfer within the meaning of term 'income'. The forgoing of premium on the part of the Petitioner amounts to extinguishment / relinquishment of a right to receive fair market value and Clauses (c) and (e) of the Explanation (i) to Section 92B of the Act: The meaning of international transaction as given would include even capital account transaction within its scope.

A conjoint reading of Section 92(1) of the Act along with Section 92(2) of the Act: indicate that what is being brought to tax is not share premium but the cost incurred by the Petitioner in passing on a benefit to its holding company by issue of shares at a premium less than ALP.

The order of the TPO/DRP demonstrates that premium on issue of share is not taxable in as much as amounts received by petitioner on account of share premium have not been taxed The Petitioner itself had submitted to the jurisdiction of Chapter X of the Act by filing/submitting Form 3-CEB, declaring the ALP.

Under Act, the income is taxable when it accrues or arises or when it is deemed to accrue or arise and not only when it is received. Therefore, even if an amount is not actually received, yet in case income has arisen or deemed to arise, then the same is chargeable to tax. Thus, income forgone is also subject to tax. Chapter X of the Act is a complete code by itself and not merely a machinery provision to compute the ALP and applies wherever the ALP is to be determined by the A.O.

The passing on of benefit by the Petitioner to its holding company would fall under the head 'Income' from other sources under Section 56(1) of the Act.

In the Shell case, the tax office alleged that the company's Indian unit under-priced shares transferred to the parent by about $2.5 billion, demanding tax on the interest the Anglo-Dutch oil company would have earned.

The income-tax department had sought to add Rs. 15,220 crore to Shell India's taxable income. Shell India had issued shares to parent Shell Gas BV at Rs 10 apiece in the 2008-09 financial year. The tax department contested this valuation and estimated it at Rs. 183 per share. The difference resulting from the revaluation of shares was treated as income in the hands of Shell India.

Case Questions

1. Whether the facts and the circumstances of the case, determine the AO's proper justification in making the transfer pricing adjustment in relation to Share Price Income incurred by the taxpayer?

2. This may result in favour of or in an increase of foreign investors who seek to invest in Indian firms from the taxation point of view. Comment

3. The court decision came in favour of Shell India challenged the order of the Income Tax Appellate Tribunal, to circumvent transfer pricing norms, though it was an international transaction wherein there was no arm's length dealing between the related entities. Discuss whether the court decision is in favour of Shell India Company's reputation

4. Do you think that the TPO was right in making adjustment to valuing the shares as underpriced where the two companies transferred shares to associated entities at Book Value? Transfer pricing policy should be seriously reviewed. Comment.

5. What is the economics of transfer pricing with related to this case, and what does it mean to jurisdiction.

6. What happens if a multinational company issues shares to overseas holding company and later on issues shares to others at a premium? Will it not be passing gain without and tax on such gain?

8

Merger of ING Vysya with Kotak Mahindra Bank

A Case Study on Bank Mergers

Learning Objectives

Bank mergers were rare happenings among major corporate banks a few years ago with due restrictions to avoid monopolistic situations in the banking sector. However, with stricter norms and standardization in bank rates in lending and deposits, the scope of competitions for attracting borrowers of funds for business and other reasons became extremely limited and some banks could not manage performance parameters which over a period of time tended to be financially sick and inoperative till such time the bank found big borrower for projects, etc. they managed purely on goodwill of loyal customers for some time.

Madura Bank was one such bank that was once a successful bank in south India but over time became sick and needed capital for normal operations even. Kotak Mahindra Bank under the stewardship of Mr. Kotak was on lookout for expanding its operations in South India which they felt had huge potential for banking operations. This led to the merger proposal and eventual merger of Madura Bank with Kotak Mahindra Bank. The case explains the process and synergies due to such bank mergers in the Indian banking industry.

Synopsis

The case study is about the merger deal between ING Vysya Bank and Kotak Mahindra Bank. The deal created the fourth largest private sector

Indian Business Case Studies. Varsha Parab, Ramesh Mahadik, and Diksha Tripathi, Oxford University Press.
© ASM Group of Institutes, Pune, India 2022. DOI: 10.1093/oso/9780192869432.003.0008

bank in the Indian banking industry. The case provides enough material to discuss the dynamics and the mergers in the Indian banking industry. The case also provides enough material to analyse and discuss the synergies and challenges of the merger deal of ING Vysya and Kotak Mahindra bank.

Case Details

In November 2014, Kotak Mahindra Bank Limited (Kotak) announced its acquisition of ING Vysya Bank Limited (ING Vysya), a quasi-foreign bank owned by Dutch multinational, the ING Group in a full-share deal worth US$2.4 billion. The deal, the biggest in the Indian banking sector, created the fourth largest private bank in India with a balance sheet size of Rs. 2 trillion and market capitalization of over Rs. 1 trillion. According to industry experts, this deal helped Kotak to expand its presence in India and to compete with other top-notch private sector players in the Indian banking industry.

The amalgamation is subject to the approval of the shareholders of Kotak and ING Vysya, respectively, Reserve Bank of India under the Banking Regulation Act, the Competition Commission of India, and such other regulatory approvals as may be required. Upon obtaining all approvals, when the merger becomes effective, ING Vysya will merge with Kotak. Shareholders of ING Vysya will receive shares of Kotak in exchange for shares in ING Vysya at the approved share exchange ('swap') ratio. All shareholders of Kotak and ING Vysya will participate thereafter in the (merged) Kotak business.

All ING Vysya branches and employees will become Kotak branches and employees. ING Vysya's CEO designate, Mr. Uday Sareen, will be inducted into the top management of Kotak, reporting directly to Mr. Uday Kotak, executive vice-chairman and managing director of Kotak. According to experts, the Indian banking sector needed such mergers not only to create world-sized banks to compete with foreign banks but also to create banks with a sufficient capital base to fund various large infrastructure projects crucial to maintain the growth of Indian economy.

However, industry experts had doubts on the synergies of the merger. They quoted a study by KPMG and Wharton, which found 83% of mergers and acquisitions (M&A) failed to produce any benefits and over half of M&A ended up reducing shareholder value instead of increasing it. Some experts were worried about the various challenges the merger deal threw up, such as the cultural differences between the two banks and the reaction of the employees union among others. However, other experts were positive about the deal.

Indian Banking Industry

Since ancient times, an indigenous banking industry had prevailed in India with some communities being traditionally involved. These communities mostly ran huge businesses apart from the banking business. In fact, the banking business was relatively smaller than their other businesses. They mainly dealt in money lending, did not accept deposits from customers, and discouraged savings.

'They used their personal wealth and that of their ancestors and income from other businesses for lending purposes. They lent money for personal as well as business purposes and were infamous for the high rates of interest they charged and their unconventional banking practices'.

M&A Activity in Indian Banking Sector

The western type of banks came into the picture in the late 18th century in India when Bank of Hindustan was established in 1770 in Calcutta (now Kolkata) in Western India. Later, General Bank of India was established in 1786 in Calcutta. Calcutta became the centre of banking activities mainly due to the trading activities of the British Empire. In the nineteenth century, the major development in the Indian banking industry was the establishment of three presidency banks by the British East India Company. However, in 1921, these three presidency banks were amalgamated to create the Imperial Bank of India.

The Indian banking sector did not witness too many M&A activities when compared to western and other countries. After the first stage of nationalization in 1969, only 34 mergers took place in the Indian banking sector. In 26 of these deals, Public Sector Banks (PSBs) acquired private sector banks that were on the brink of failure, mostly on a directive from the RBI. The remaining eight deals happened between private sector banks.

The merger prior to the Kotak and ING Vysya merger in the private sector banking space took place in 2010 when Bank of Rajasthan merged with ICICI Bank in a US$398 million deal. There were many reasons for the low number of M&As in India. These included restrictive regulations, a major part of the banking industry being owned by the Indian government, and the rigid resistance by strong employees unions.

About Kotak

Kotak started as a non-banking financial company (NBFC)—Kotak Mahindra Capital Management Finance Limited (KMCMFL)—in 1985 in India. KMCMFL was renamed Kotak Mahindra Finance Limited (KMFL) in 1985 and it received its banking license in February 2003 to become the first NBFC to be converted into a full-fledged private bank in India. It was renamed as Kotak Mahindra Bank Limited (Kotak).

The consolidated balance sheet of Kotak Mahindra Group is over Rs. 1.34 lakh crores and the consolidated net worth of the Group stands at Rs. 20,554 crore (approx. US$3.3 billion) as on 30 September 2014. The Group offers a wide range of financial services that encompass every sphere of life. From commercial banking to stock broking, mutual funds, life insurance, and investment banking, the Group caters to the diverse financial needs of individuals and the corporate sector. The Group has a wide distribution network through branches and franchisees across India, and international offices in London, New York, Dubai, Abu Dhabi, Mauritius, and Singapore.

Kotak Mahindra Bank

Kotak Mahindra Bank (KMB) offers complete retail financial solutions for varied customer requirements. The savings bank account goes beyond the traditional role of savings and provides a wide range of services through a comprehensive suite of investment services and other transactional conveniences like Online Shopping, Bill Payments, ASBA, Netc@rd, ActivMoney (automatic TD sweep-in and sweep-out), etc. Kotak's Jifi, a first-of-its-kind fully integrated Social Bank Account, redefines digital banking by seamlessly incorporating social networking platforms like Twitter and Facebook with mainstream banking. KayPay, the world's first bank agnostic payment product for Facebook users, enables millions of bank account holders to transfer money to each other at any hour of the day or night, without the need of net banking or knowing various bank account related details of the payee.

KMBL also offers an investment account where mutual fund investments are recorded and can be viewed in a consolidated fashion across fund houses and schemes. Further, the bank offers loan products such as home loans, personal loans, commercial vehicle loans, etc. Keeping in mind the diverse needs of the business community, KMBL offers comprehensive business solutions that include current account, trade services, cash management services, and credit facilities.

About ING Vysya Bank

ING Vysya was incorporated as Vysya Bank Limited (Vysya Bank) in 1930 in Bangalore, Karnataka, in Southern India. In 2002, ING Vysya came into existence when the ING Group acquired a major stake in Vysya Bank. This was the first acquisition of an Indian bank by any foreign bank. ING Vysya offered various financial services under four business segments—treasury, corporate/wholesale banking, retail banking, and other banking operations.

At the end of FY14, ING Vysya had generated revenue of Rs. 60.72 billion with a net profit of Rs. 6.58 billion. ING Vysya Bank Ltd is a premier private sector bank with retail, private and wholesale banking platforms that serve over two million customers. With over 80 years of history in India and leveraging ING's global financial expertise, the bank offers a broad range of innovative and established products and services across its 573 branches.

The bank, which has close to 10,000 employees, is also listed in Bombay Stock Exchange Limited and National Stock Exchange of India Limited. ING Vysya Bank was ranked among top five most trusted brands among private sector banks in India in the Economic Times

Brand Equity—Nielsen survey 2011. ING is a global financial institution of Dutch origin offering banking services through its operating company ING Bank and holds significant stakes in listed insurers NN Group NV and Voya Financial, Inc. ING Bank's 53,000 employees offer retail and commercial banking services to customers in over 40 countries.

Merger Deal

On 20 November 2014, Kotak announced the merger with ING Vysya in an all-stock deal worth Rs. 148.51 billion or US$2.4 billion. On regulatory approval, all of ING Vysya's branches and businesses would merge with Kotak. ING Vysya's shareholders would get 0.725 share of Kotak stock for every one stock of ING Vysya they held, i.e. 725 shares of Kotak for every 1,000 shares of ING Vysya. This exchange ratio indicated that the implied price of each stock of ING Vysya was Rs. 790, which was based on the average stock price of Kotak and ING Vysya for one month—from 20 October 2014 to 19 November 2014—which came to Rs. 1089.50 and Rs. 682, respectively.

1. Stock swap: Deals can be conducted in cash or by exchange shares. The Kotak-ING Vysya deal will purely be an exchange of stocks. Investors in ING Vysya will get 725 Kotak Mahindra Bank shares for every 1,000 ING Vysya shares they held. This means every Kotak share is worth nearly 1.4 shares of ING Vysya. The deal values each share of ING Vysya at Rs. 790, much lower than its Thursday closing price of Rs. 816.95. However, it is 16% more than the average share price of the ING stock. This means Kotak is paying slightly more than the market price to buy the smaller bank. The entire deal would be valued at over Rs. 15,000 crores or $2.4 billion, one of the largest ever.

2. Fourth biggest private bank: The acquisition will create the fourth largest private sector bank in India in terms of the branch network. The combined entity will have a market capitalization of Rs 1 lakh crore. This is lower than the market capitalizations of HDFC Bank (Rs 2.2 lakh crores), ICICI Bank (Rs 1.98 lakh crores) and Axis Bank (Rs 1.14 lakh crores)—three of the largest private sector banks in India.

3. Shareholding: Uday Kotak will remain to be the key promoter, holding around 34% stake in the merged bank. This is down from 40%. As per shareholding rules, he has to reduce his stake further to 20% over the next four years. Dutch lender ING Groep NV will be the second-largest shareholder in the new Kotak Mahindra bank after the deal. It held a nearly 43% stake in ING Vysya. Its shareholding in the new entity would be nearly 25.3%, according to an Economic Times report. (ET Prime)

4. Brokerages give thumbs up: Most analysts and brokerage firms cheered the deal. This is because they expect the deal to improve Kotak Mahindra's bank business by expanding its branch network as well as improving its loan portfolio. The deal also happens at a time when the economy is showing signs of improvement. This means Kotak will be in a better position to take advantage of any rise in demand for loans, analysts said. The deal is likely to increase Kotak's loan book by nearly two-thirds (75%), brokerages said.

5. Branch network: The merger is expected to double Kotak's branch network from 641 to 1,214 having nearly 40,000 employees. ING Vysya currently has about 573 branches in the country, most of which are situated in the South. This is good news is because Kotak was predominantly present in North India. This means the two bank's branches do not overlap. The merger also means the combined entity will have a far wider reach in the country than earlier. Kotak is expected to gain 2 million customers from the merger.

6. SME banking: ING Vysya also brings its SME banking platform to the table. This will help Kotak in the long run. As of September 2014, ING Vysya lent about 70% of its total loans to small and medium enterprises (SME) and large companies. In contrast, Kotak lent only 55%. The merger is thus likely to strengthen Kotak's corporate lending business. All of this is expected to increase Kotak's total earnings by one-fifth or 20%, experts suggest.

7. First profitable bank merger since 2008: The banking sector rarely sees a lot of mergers and acquisitions. This is because of strict rules which restrict such movements. Since the 2008 banking crisis, there have been only two deals. However, both the deals involved a profitable bank taking over a smaller loss-making entity. The Kotak Mahindra–ING Vysya deal will be the first since 2008 involving two profit-making banks.

The merger increased the geographical presence and further deepened Kotak's network, thanks to the complementary network of ING Vysya. The merger increased Kotak's number of branches and its ATMs network by 47% and 35% to 1,214 and 1,794, respectively. Before the merger, 80% of Kotak's branches were in the western and northern parts of the country and only 15% were in the southern part of India. On the other hand, ING Vysya had a greater presence in the southern part of the country with 64% of its branches located there and only 32% of its branches in the western and northern parts of the country. After the merger, Kotak had a balanced presence in different parts of the country.

The major challenge was related to human resource management. The salary structure of both banks was also quite different. Around one-third employees of the 10,591 employees of ING Vysya were unionized and their pay structure came under the Indian Banks Association. The employees of ING Vysya were worried whether their pay structure would continue or not. Some of the employees of ING Vysya had other concerns too. Employees in positions like regional manager, sales head, zonal manager, etc., were apprehensive that duplication of positions could lead to transfers or even to their losing their jobs.

According to experts, completing the deal under the nose of the employees' union was the big challenge for Kotak as the employees had already threatened to go on strike on the issue. In 2009, a merger deal between Federal Bank and Catholic Syrian Bank Ltd. did not go through due to the employees union. The troubles for Kotak were compounded when the Securities and Exchange Board of India (SEBI) started an investigation into unusual trading in the shares of Kotak and ING Vysya before the merger was announced in November 2014.

Case Questions

1. Discuss and debate whether the merger deal between Kotak and ING Vysya would help the Indian banking industry.

2. Discuss the synergies of the merger between ING Vysya and Kotak.

3. Understand the challenges faced by the merged Kotak going forward and explore the ways in which it can overcome these challenges.

9

Delayed Wisdom

A Case Study on Likely Issues in the BIC (Bankruptcy and Insolvency Code)

Learning Objectives

The much-awaited Bankruptcy and Insolvency Code was introduced as one of the major financial reforms by the Government of India, one concerned to be a highly progressive step to release the immense financial strain the creditors have been under skyrocketing debts of the customer and huge unpaid overdue bills of its suppliers and creditors. BIC as is popularly known was supposed to work as an antidote for stuck-up cash flows and empty bank coffers engulfed by humungous NPAs stuck up as advances and loans to failed businesses.

Initially, BIC had a good impact in identifying bankrupt and insolvent business ventures and insisting on compliance to its provisions of disposal of revivable assets of Insolvent companies by financial buy over bids by investors capable and interested in the take over the debts along with revivable assets and the creditors' liabilities settled through the BIC provisions.

There have been some evasive efforts by a few companies to get under the provisions of BIC and encourage like-minded investors to bid for the takeover. While we need to be careful in naming such attempts to by-pass the real purpose of BIC in order to get rid of near-dead business and make a back door entry by associating with a few bidders and attempting to recapture the once failed business.

At times the promoters have come back and made fresh bids for stoppage of takeover by offering improved offers to settle the arrears of debts of the business. This was, however, disallowed by the regulators of BIC but the question remains as to why in the first instance, the erstwhile

Indian Business Case Studies. Varsha Parab, Ramesh Mahadik, and Diksha Tripathi, Oxford University Press.
© ASM Group of Institutes, Pune, India 2022. DOI: 10.1093/oso/9780192869432.003.0009

promoter did not make an improved plan of repayment of debts? A delayed wisdom or fear of losing related subsidiaries in case the rival bidder is threatening to destabilize the subsidiaries as well.

The case provides an interesting insight into likely issues in the effective implementation of the BIC. In fact, the Case author has offered his opinions posing relevant questions on the case issues.

Synopsis

Essar is short and long for S. Shashi Ruia and R. Ravi Ruia, chairman and vice-chairman of the conglomerate Essar who founded it in 1969; the company was later incorporated in 1976. With its roots in the construction of an outer breakwater in Chennai Port, the company was involved in core sectors like marine construction, pipeline laying, dredging, and other port-related activities before venturing into the core sectors like exploration and development, oil and gas, for the Indian Public Sector in 1984.

The first IPO was launched in 1988 under the name of Essar Offshore and Exploration listed both in the Bombay Stock Exchange and the Indian Stock Exchange. The 1990s marked Essar's entry into steelmaking with its Hazira plant in Gujarat and a pellet plant in Visakhapatnam.

The new vertical in the iron and steel sector was part of a restructuring plan, with a new business strategy that 'hived off' it's unrelated business to various different companies. The 1992 saw the construction of a technology *Hot Rolled* sheets and coils plant in Hazira, in the western state of Gujarat with the renaming of Essar Gujarat Limited to Essar Steel Limited in the year 1995 with a capacity measuring a million tonnes annually.

Essar Steel, a completely integrated steel producer, from iron ore to market-ready steel products with ore beneficiation, pellet making, iron making, steel making, and downstream facilities including cold rolling mill, galvanizing, pre-coated facility, steel processing facility, extra wide plate mill and a pipe mill in between, had a 10 million tonnes annual capacity. ESSAR Steel India Limited made its foray into foreign countries with Essar Steel Minnesota LLC, a company located in the US State of Minnesota, Greenfield projects in Vietnam, a steel plant in Indonesia, and an integrated steel plant in Trinidad and Tobago. It has a current capacity of 10 MTPA which they plan to raise to 20 MTPA by 2028.

The first signs of financial disease were revealed to the public with the naming of Essar Steel in a list of 12 defaulters by the Reserve Bank of India (RBI) in the June of 2017. RBI requested the respective lending banks to begin insolvency proceedings against the company under the Insolvency and Bankruptcy Act, 2016 and this is the way the company stood in a legal and financial dispute with Rs. 54,547 crores of debt till the recent reversals.

The Road to Descent

Essar Steel had struggled with elevated debt levels since it had defaulted on a loan in 1999, before turning around in 2002/03. The company again went through a difficult phase during 2011–2014 and was at the bottom of the pit among its peers. Its debt level on a standalone basis was higher than other private sector steelmakers; its sales had grown at the slowest pace and it posted losses in four out of seven years since 2007/08. In comparison, Tata Steel, JSW Steel, and Jindal Steel and Power did not post losses during that period. By 2013/14, Essar Steel had amassed a whopping Rs. 37,559 crores in consolidated debt, and its interest payout in servicing stood at Rs. 4,580 crores during the year.

While this had initially made bankers reluctant to cater to its working capital needs of Rs. 4,000 crores to fund the ambitious revival plan, the $35 billion Essar Group's backing helped it bag the much-needed cash. Essar also had similar issues with Algoma. After an infusion of $300 million by the Group, the Algoma unit refinanced its liabilities and deleveraged its balance sheet by $200 million. It also reduced its cash interest by $47 million. The measures helped Algoma post a profit of CDN$26.8 million in the third quarter of 2013/14, compared with a net loss of CDN$38.6 million a year earlier.

The slowdown in China, the world's largest consumer of the alloy, as well as rising inventories and falling global steel prices, added to the company's woes. The other reasons were internal to the company. In 2007, the company charted an aggressive plan to triple its production capacity to 25 million tonnes by 2012 in Asia (including India) and North America.

The plans went awry after the collapse of Lehman Brothers and the subsequent 2008 recession in the following year, sending shockwaves through the global economy and roiling the commodities markets. Shares of top global steelmakers, such as ArcelorMittal and Tata Steel, lost as much as four-fifths of their value, and the industry started at a bleak future.

At a time when prudence should have been the watchword, Essar Steel continued to borrow to fund its aggressive growth plans. Between 2007/08 and 2013/14, the company's debt soared five-fold while its sales grew only 20%. Its 2007 acquisition of Canadian steelmaker Algoma for $1.5 billion also proved to be challenging with the unit filing for bankruptcy protection in July 2014. 'The company failed to react quickly to the economic volatility during the time of expansion,' says Vinayak S. Bapat, president and CEO, VXL Consulting. in the market.

Regulatory hurdles at home, curb on industrial gas allocation, and unavailability of raw material during the past four years also proved to be a bane that Essar Steel could do without. The fall in gas production at the Krishna–Godavari Basin, which affected the overall availability of gas in the country, prompted the Centre to give priority to city gas distribution over industrial use. Essar Steel's gas-based production capacity at Hazira in Gujarat took a hit, with 6.8 mt of the total capacity of 10 mt shutting down.

The company's backward integration plans, too, suffered due to a three-year delay in getting regulatory approvals for the 253 km long slurry pipeline connecting the beneficiation plant at Dabuna to the pellet plant at Paradip in Odisha. 'The operational costs would have come down by 15 per cent if backward integration had been completed on time,' says an analyst. However, industry executives are not convinced. 'The situation was same across steel companies. But Essar was less aggressive in production and sales.'

ESL—Rudderless Ship?

Ruia's entered the steel business in 1992 and ESL—a completely integrated vertical handling from iron ore to market-ready products–was in place by 1995. While ESL was doing fairly well, as were the other players in the steel industry till 2007/08. ESL embarked on an aggressive expansion plan, needless to add, highly leveraged during 2007/08 through 2013/14. This period was characterized by 'Lehman shock', falling commodity markets, value loss (falling market cap) of major global players in the steel industry.

Legal Process—Timeline

Government of India passed the act, namely Insolvency & Bankruptcy Code, 2016 (IBC)—a bankruptcy law was passed in 2016 and sought to consolidate the existing framework by creating a single law for insolvency and bankruptcy. The IBC is, in fact, a one-stop solution to resolve insolvencies which previously was a long process that did not offer an economically viable arrangement/solution.

ESL, a major loan default, was an acid test of IBC in seeking a successful resolution to insolvency cases.

June 2017: RBI names ESL as a defaulter amongst 12 major defaulters and asks the lenders to commence insolvency proceedings under the newly enacted Insolvency & Bankruptcy Regulation Act of 2016 (IBR) in the matter of outstanding default loan of Rs. 54,547 crores.

July 2017: Consortium of the banks refers ESL for insolvency proceedings at National Company Law Tribunal (NCLT) of Ahmedabad judicature.

August 2017: NCLT admits proceedings.

October 2017: Five metal giants submit an expression of interest for ESL.

November 2017: GOI amend IBC to introduce Section 29 (A), which precludes owners or owner relates interests from participating in the bidding. A major flaw in IBC was corrected.

January 2018: NuMetal was formed in Mauritius with Ruia family participation (minority holding) to participate in ESL bidding process.

February 2018: Arcelor Mittal, Luxembourg (AM) and NuMetal, Mauritius (NM), submit a final bid for ESL.

March 2018: Lenders reject both the bids.

April 2018: AM and NM challenge the bid rejection with NCLT and NCLT asks lenders to reconsider the bids.

September 2018: NCLT allows NM to bid and asks AM to clear default debts of Uttam Galva and KSS Petron (both Indian subsidiaries of AM) amounting to Rs. 900 crores.

October 2018: AM files petition in the Supreme Court of India (SC) challenging the NCLT decision. SC rules both bidders to be ineligible unless they clear their pending debts.

October 2018: AM clears the dues (circa Rs. 9,000 crores) and revises the bid to Rs. 42,000 crores (note: increases the AM bid by Rs. 9,000 crores on the revised bid of Rs. 42,000 crores, i.e. AM Group level cost of acquisition stands at Rs. 51,000 crores).

January 2019: Ruia's offer to settle the entire debt (substantially lacking in details as to means and plans for repayment), NCLT rejects the offer.

March 2019: NCLT approves AM bid.

A twist in the story—subordinated operational creditors *(credits are unsecured)* wish to have a share in the pie and request NCLT to give them a share in proceeds along with senior debt holders *(debts are fully secured and have priority to apportion the proceeds towards the debt repayment).*

July 2019: NCLT asks lenders to give more funds to operational creditors without recognizing the senior or subordinate debts. Lenders summarily discard the NCLT proposal.

November 2019: SC rules, the hierarchy of creditors to be followed and lenders to have the final say.

December 2019: GOI amends IBC and offers protection to buyers from criminal investigations into an acquisition deal by the promoters (note: hostile acquisition with criminal intent OR promoters to start new litigations to bar the acquirers of their assets).

December 2019: AM signs the closure documentation and assets are handed over to AM.

Long Process, Deterioration of the Asset and Loss of Its Value to Lenders–Interim Measures

The legal course took two and a half years to resolve. It's a long period. Financially stressed assets (ESL) need special attention as they degrade over a period of time and value deteriorates exponentially. It was therefore imperative for lenders to appoint 'turnaround managers' who would scale up production, focus on cost reduction, keep ESL products visible in the markets, expand VAP range, and ensure adequate liquidity.

Alvarez & Marsal's name was insisted by the private sector banks for quality reasons and was opposed by PSU banks for cost reasons. However, quality argument prevailed over the cost argument and Alvarez & Marsel were chosen as turnaround agents.

The first job was to get the interim finance in place for the working capital needs of ESL. Their request to lender consortium for short-term financing of Rs. 1,500 to 2,000 crores was turned down and they had to turn to vendors for extending their services with longer credit terms; though it was a more expensive financing form, the job was done (they followed *peking order*).

The next was shielding the ESL from inter-connectedness with other Ruia group companies. While Ruia's were mounting legal measures against bankruptcy proceedings, they did not disrupt the operations of ESL (note: promoters hoping to get back the control of the asset would not attempt to damage it as undoing costs much more in terms of efforts and money if the control of the asset is regained).

With ESL defaulting, the consortium of banks had put 'cash monitoring system' in the place where they could trace cash flows and link receipts and payments so that funds are not misappropriated. This helped Alvarez & Marsel in controlling the ESL cash flows efficiently.

Banks were earlier 'tagging' the funds (the cash inflows were tagged/applied to outstanding obligations). Alvarez & Marsel managed to stop funds tagging by the banks and free more cash to the extent of Rs. 200 to 250 crores. Lenders were initially unhappy but they agreed (note: this became a norm in subsequent insolvency proceedings). External factors like falling energy prices, recovery of steel prices led to better cash flows.

Production rose from 5.47 million tons (2017) to 6.78 million tons (2019). More importantly, a successful asset preservation/turnaround exercise helped financial creditors. AM carried out three due diligence exercises and an initial bid of Rs. 29,000 crores was raised to Rs. 42,000 crores in the final round (not to forget, AM also paid the default obligations of Rs. 9,000 crores of their Indian subsidiaries). However, AM, in turn, acquired a world-class steel plant with a capacity of 10 million TPA which was producing, profitable, and cash generating at lower than the replacement cost.

Case Questions

1. Timing of an aggressive expansion decision–was that right? Why did ESL not abort the growth plan, especially when it was highly leveraged?

Comments:
Higher fixed costs, especially debt servicing costs, mounted during this period and thus the bottom line was hypersensitive to a small change in the top line. During this period of seven years, gross sales of ESL moved up from Rs. 11,911 crores to Rs. 14,352 crores, PAT went down from Rs. 429 crores to a loss of Rs. 1,597 crores and debts went up five-fold from Rs. 6,261 crores to Rs. 31,421 crores, whereas industry competitor Tata Steel mustered the gross sales growth from Rs. 22,110 crores to Rs. 46,309 crores, PAT—from Rs. 4,687 crores to Rs. 6,412 crores and debt increase from Rs. 19,093 crores to Rs. 27,917 crores (note: debt/sales, NP margins are much inferior as compared to TS).

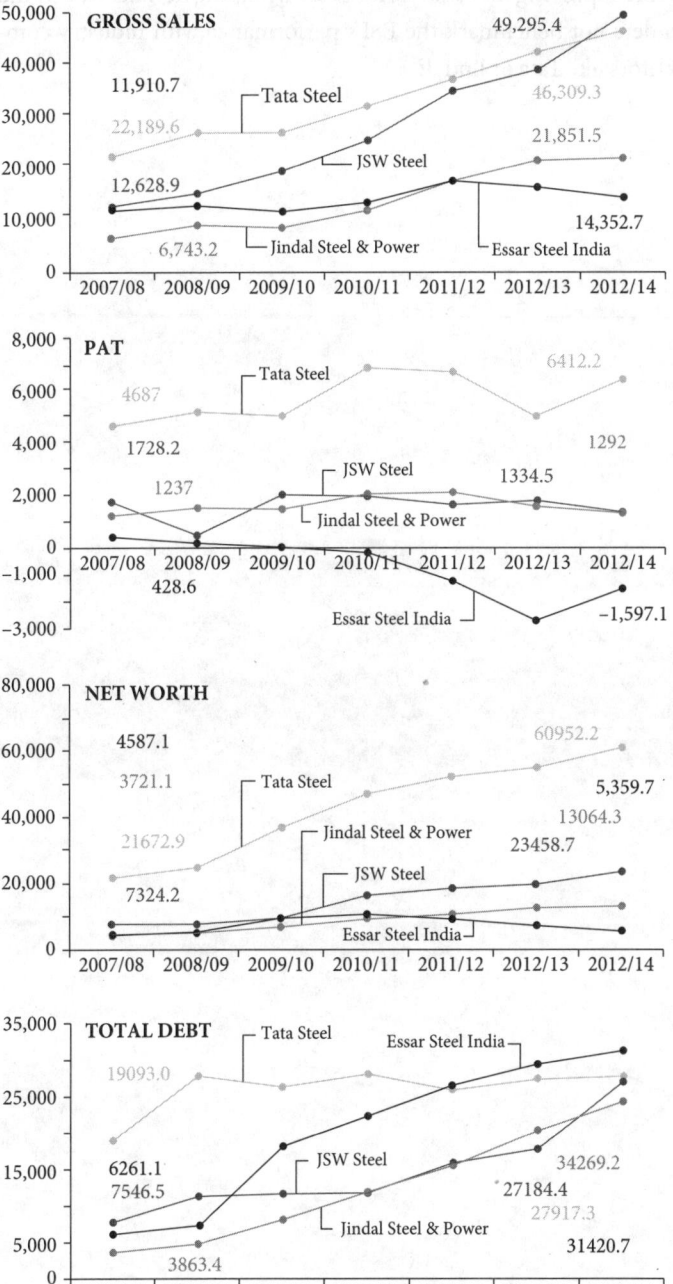

2. While approving the requests for ever-increasing new debts, why did lenders not benchmark the ESL's performance with industry competitors like Tata or Jindal?

10

Global Economies and Crude Oil Prices

A Case Study in Geo Politics

Learning Objectives

The common factor resulting in fluctuation in prices of crude oil are expected to follow the normal demand and supply situations. But on many occasions, the Organization of the Petroleum-Exporting Countries (OPEC) countries deliberately create situations leading to short supplies and resulting price increases which in many oil-consuming economies also create resistance to power centres to bring down the prices.

Now one more aspect threatening to impact oil consumption is the climate and pollution control rules resulting in shifting over to lower or less polluting fuels such as solar, electric, and wind powers hence OPEC countries are worried of steeper falls in crude oil demands during the next few years and in order to maintain supply channels busy through reduced crude oil prices.

The crude oil price fluctuations have a sudden and severe impact on oil-exporting countries' economies. Some countries have nearly 75 to 80% of their GDPs dependent on oil exports and need to closely monitor movements in crude oil prices to avoid economic blackout.

The students' studies in business economies will learn a few strategies adopted by OPEC countries in not allowing economic downfall due mainly to fluctuations in crude oil prices.

Synopsis

Oil and gas prices are as always volatile and unpredictable. In 2008, for instance, oil hit a high of $145 a barrel. But that didn't last long. And in 2015,

Indian Business Case Studies. Varsha Parab, Ramesh Mahadik, and Diksha Tripathi, Oxford University Press.
© ASM Group of Institutes, Pune, India 2022. DOI: 10.1093/oso/9780192869432.003.0010

despite all sorts of turmoil in the Middle East and in other oil-producing countries like Nigeria, the price of crude fell between 30% and 40% to its lowest levels in 11 years. That's a bigger drop than the commodity price declines for metals, grains, and soybeans. Gas stations around the United States didn't fully reflect this drop, but petrol prices still fell to an average of $2.40 a gallon, saving each driver more than $500 last year.

There are a number of reasons for the price drop, but it boils down to supply (more of it) and demand (less of it). The United States boosted oil production by 66% over the last five years, making it the largest oil and natural gas producer in the world in 2015. Other producers, like Saudi Arabia, also didn't scale back, in part to stick it to a sanctions-hobbled Iran and snatch up its clients. Meanwhile, greater fuel efficiency and slower economic growth around the world (particularly in China) have reduced demand. The nosedive in oil prices has been good news for a lot of people and a lot of countries. But it's not good news for the planet.

First the Good News

Consumers love lower energy prices. It's not only cheaper to fill up the tank and heat the house. Your shopping bill is also smaller because of lower manufacturing and transportation costs. Airlines cut fares (or at least they should). And it's a big boost for the global economy. As *The Economist* notes, 'a price fall normally boosts GDP by shifting resources from producers to consumers, who are more likely to spend their gains than wealthy sheikhdoms'.

The other good news is that lower oil prices haven't undercut the market for sustainable energy. In the past, cheaper fossil fuels have meant that governments and industry put off the hard decision to shift to renewable energy sources. But several factors have changed this calculus.

The international community has made a commitment, most recently in Paris, to invest in wind turbines and solar panels. Because of technological advances and government incentives, meanwhile, the cost of renewables has fallen.

The price of solar panels in the United States, for instance, has dropped 70% since 2009, and industry observers expect even sharper cuts in the years ahead. To keep up the momentum, the Obama administration pushed through an extension until 2019 of its tax credits encouraging renewable energy. And the investment banks, usually risk-averse on this issue, are finally betting big on the sector: Goldman Sachs, for instance, announced in November that it would increase investments in renewable energy by fourfold.

Another environmental benefit to lower energy prices is the cancellation of pricier fossil fuel projects. President Obama finally deep-sixed the Keystone pipeline last November. The target of heated activist protest, the pipeline had become a considerably less attractive project when oil prices fell below $60 a barrel.

The State Department is also thrilled with lower oil prices. The US allies in Europe and Asia are able to reduce their energy purchases (and free up resources to buy the US goods, including military hardware). And key US oil-producing adversaries are feeling the pinch. Iran, already under sanctions on its oil production, became more amenable last year to negotiations on its nuclear program. Russia, also under sanctions, hasn't pushed as hard in Ukraine. Lower oil prices have put pressure on Venezuela and also reduced the flow of income to the Islamic State.

Decreasing the US dependency on foreign oil through a boost in domestic production is not only a good media sound bite but also a hit with the voters. It also turns out to be a potent weapon for the US foreign policy, which is good news for battling the Islamic State but bad news for restraining arms sales.

And Now the Bad News

Much was made in December of news of a potential global 'peak' in carbon emissions. Researchers from the University of East Anglia and the Global Carbon Project released a report that greenhouse gas emissions dropped in 2015 by 0.6%. That might not seem like much. But it represented the first such reduction in decades.

Carbon emissions have been going down in the EU. They dropped a bit in the United States in 2015. But the real reason for the global dip is China. Because of its recent economic slowdown, the country used a lot less coal last year.

So, this should be good news. But it isn't. First of all, aside from China, the United States, and the EU, carbon emissions in the rest of the world continued their upward climb. Second, it's more than likely that the drop was an anomaly—just as earlier predictions of 'peak oil' proved premature.

And third, for any campaign to achieve zero emissions, cheap fossil fuels are the worst kind of disincentive. The price point is simply too irresistible—for car owners who want to go on vacation, companies that want to increase their profits, and governments that want to spur economic growth.

Geopolitical Ramifications

Saudi Arabia has recently been acting quite over the top. It intervened militarily in neighbouring Yemen to put down an insurgency it blamed on Iran (with no evidence). It's funnelled money to its own preferred insurgents (namely, Sunni extremists) to topple Bashar al-Assad in Syria. And on New Year's Day, it executed a number of 'terrorists', including Sheikh Nimr al-Nimr, a leading Shiite cleric.

Saudi Arabia, of course, is not known for its moderation. But the government in Riyadh has been acting even more erratically and paranoid than usual. Or perhaps Saudi Arabia has good reason to be paranoid. Falling oil prices mean economic trouble for a country that depends on sales of crude for 85–90% of its revenues. The country is already running a huge deficit—some 15% of GDP. In their most recent budget, the Saudis indicated that some belt-tightening is in the offing, which will translate into curtailing key subsidies like gas and water.

Reduce subsidies and prices go up. If prices go up, people get upset. In other countries in the Middle East, price hikes have resulted in protest spikes. It's no surprise, then, that Riyadh is doing what it can to eliminate potential sources of opposition at home and abroad.

Volatility in the energy market has helped to destabilize governments in the past: the Soviet Union under Gorbachev, the Suharto regime in Indonesia, or Venezuela just prior to the ascent of Hugo Chavez. So, it's not far-fetched to imagine the winds of change blowing through Saudi Arabia—or Russia, where the economic situation is edging towards desperate, or Iran, which is anxious to see the lifting of economic sanctions as a result of the nuclear deal.

But as F. Gregory Gause points out in a Brookings report from April 2015, oil prices are just one factor affecting government stability, and most oil producers have enough reserves to weather the volatility. Indeed, Gause imagined that falling oil prices might even promote greater stability in the Middle East as Iran and Saudi Arabia worked more closely to coordinate production cuts. In fact, with Saudi Arabia severing ties with Iran this week, it looks more likely that both will continue to pump oil aggressively, driving prices down even further.

It perhaps flirts with conspiracy to imagine that the United States has boosted energy production to keep prices low in order to promote unrest in Russia, or that Saudi Arabia has done the same to foster discontent in Iran. Both countries have plenty of other reasons to push the pedal to the metal, energy-wise. But policymakers in Riyadh and Washington would certainly not be upset if their strategy produced such side benefits.

The problem is that instability in Russia and Iran isn't in the best interests of either the United States or Saudi Arabia. Washington needs the help of Moscow and Tehran to negotiate a solution in Syria. And the Rouhani administration, compared to a more hardline clerical government that could easily emerge in Iran, is a much better potential negotiating partner for Saudi Arabia (assuming, of course, that it even wants a negotiating partner).

A Golden Opportunity

Low energy prices have come along at a particularly opportune time. Governments can't sit back and expect the market to allocate resources wisely, especially when it comes to the environment. That investments are flowing into the renewable sector despite the dip in oil and natural gas prices is about all the luck we can count on. It's not clear how long prices will remain low. During this period, governments must use the savings wisely. Priority number one should be the removal of energy subsidies.

Energy subsidies, which amount to more than $540 billion per year worldwide, are as common as they are damaging to economies, the poor, and the environment, since they stimulate consumption and undermine efforts to save energy and use it more efficiently.

According to the World Bank, these subsidies are highly regressive: As much as 60 or even 80% of what governments in the Middle East and North Africa spend to subsidize energy benefits the richest 20% of the population, with the poor receiving less than 10% of these public funds. With prices so low, governments can more easily phase out these energy subsidies without causing as much disruption for consumers (while providing cash transfers to help the most disadvantaged).

The second priority is for governments to use the windfall from cheaper energy imports to provide a different kind of subsidy: for renewables. This is the moment when the world must take a sharp turn. Governments should focus on the public sector: reducing the carbon footprint of government buildings, schools, hospitals, and so on. But they must also make it economically irresistible for households to go solar, for utilities to build wind farms, and for businesses to make manufacturing more efficient.

The third priority is counter-intuitive. Energy producers must come together to reduce production. This will ultimately lead to higher oil and gas prices. But that is as it should be. If we are to achieve carbon neutrality, we have to make fossil fuels as expensive as possible.

The former Venezuelan oil minister Juan Pablo Perez Alfonso, a driving force behind the creation of the OPEC, wasn't interested in raising gas prices in order to collect windfall profits. An environmentalist of sorts, he considered petroleum 'the devil's excrement'. He saw OPEC—and its ability to cut production and boost prices—as a tool for conservation.

Conclusions

Geopolitics is used as a method of foreign policy. The advantages of WTO to some global economies for global governance are due to natural resources. While in some economies this has created a huge gap between wealth distribution and economic activities. Crude oil and international monetary/financial system are affected in the reverse direction but in equal % wef 2006 and 2016, i.e. about 55% decline in crude oil price and the Indian rupee in USD terms.

Case Questions

1. Will oil boil or roil in the near future in the world economic system?

2. Is it that oil slicks have made the floor slippery for the world's financial market?

SECTION III

MULTIDISCIPLINARY CASE STUDIES IN MARKETING, STRATEGY, OPERATIONS

Marketing Management, Strategic Management Mergers and Acquisitions, and Operations Strategy

11

The Agni Pariksha

A Case Study on Maruti Suzuki Ltd—The Largest Passenger Car Manufacturer in India

Learning Objectives

Larger organization like Maruti Suzuki manufacturing and selling maximum number of cars in the Domestic markets and exports as well need to handle their human resources so meticulously that there are no impending serious issues while aiming at maximum cooperation and productivity from the floor level employees.

To a great extent, companies succeed in generating max support and participation in maxmization of productivity and enabling maximum sales of their products. But changing circumstances including major expansions in capacity calls for stabling new factories in different locations. At these new plants as per local situations governing employment preferences is the condition of employing maximum number from surrounding locations.

Companies, on the other hand, need to expedite the start of regular operations at the new location due to pressure of maximum supplies from the new plant on priority. This at times leads to the transfer of few experts from the previous locations and many at the new plant lack the necessary skills and experience in jacking up productivity comparable to mother plants.

Hence new categories of employees such as temporary or contract labour need to be engaged. This is exactly where the IR relations get disturbed and if not handled in time, lead to serious skirmishes and misunderstanding between the local management and workers through their strong unions.

Indian Business Case Studies. Varsha Parab, Ramesh Mahadik, and Diksha Tripathi, Oxford University Press.
© ASM Group of Institutes, Pune, India 2022. DOI: 10.1093/oso/9780192869432.003.0011

Synopsis

Maruti Suzuki company has faced violent and disturbing labour unions, which have ransacked the running company, damaging property, and intimidating senior management executives through violent activities including causing physical harm.

The Case Study deals with detailing out what really caused the initial breakdown of IR relations and consequent dangerous development of violent strikes by labour unions and the resolutary steps taken by the management.

Case Details

Suzuki Motor Corporation of Japan will set up a plant in Gujarat to manufacture cars for its Indian unit, Maruti Suzuki India. The fully owned subsidiary, Suzuki Motor Gujarat Pvt Ltd, will have a paid-up capital of Rs. 100 crores and be in place by April 2017.

Maruti Suzuki India's board has approved the proposal, which is expected to result in substantial financial benefits for the company and its minority shareholders. However, the stock market did not take kindly to the announcement and Maruti Suzuki's shares fell 8 per cent to close at Rs. 1,563.20 on the Bombay Stock Exchange.

Maruti Suzuki had proposed setting up a car plant in Gujarat, for which it acquired about 1,200 acres in the Mehsana district. The company had also signed an agreement with the State Government to set up a plant with an annual capacity of 250,000 units with an initial investment of about Rs. 4,000 crore.

'This (Suzuki Motor Gujarat—SMGPL) will not be a public listed company. It will only be a manufacturing entity. All the marketing and expansion of the dealer network will be taken care of by MSIL (Maruti Suzuki) and, in return, all three entities Suzuki Motor Corp, MSIL and SMGPL will share the profits', declared Osamu Suzuki, Chairman, Suzuki Motor Corporation Japan.

The Gujarat plant will start operations in 2017 and roll out vehicles from early 2018, the company said. The cost of the new plant is estimated at Rs. 4,000 crore in the first phase (till 2017), and this expenditure will now be incurred by Suzuki Motor. However, owner-ship of the land will remain with Maruti, which will, in turn, lease it out to Suzuki Motor.

The Japanese parent said it would also continue to fully support Maruti's existing plants in Gurgaon and Manesar, Haryana. In add-ition, the upcoming research and development centre in Rohtak, also in Haryana, will be under Maruti. The Suzuki subsidiary would not sell vehicles to anybody else, said R. C. Bhargava, chairman, Maruti Suzuki. The company would benefit because the vehicles would be sold without any return on capital employed, Bhargava said, adding that Maruti would avoid all risks inherent to any investment.

Higher Localization, Cost Reduction Drive
Maruti Suzuki

'Higher localization, favourable foreign exchange, and a cost reduc-tion initiative by the company contributed significantly to the net profit', the carmaker said. However, net sales dropped 3 per cent to Rs. 10,619 crore from Rs. 10,956 crore. Vehicle sales during the quarter also dropped 4.4 per cent to 2.88 lakh units (3.01 lakh units) and remained under stress during the period, in both domestic and export markets. According to analysts, the company reported stronger-than-expected results. 'While the top line was broadly in line with our estimates, bottom line at Rs681 crore was higher than our estimates of Rs. 620 crore due to better-than-expected EBITDA margins at 12.4 per cent', said Yaresh Kothari, Research Analyst at Angel Broking.

Why Investors Shunned Maruti Stock?

Despite a 36 per cent growth in net profit in the December 2013 quarter over the corresponding period last year, investor concerns on Maruti Suzuki India's plans for its Gujarat plant saw the company's stock lose 8 per cent after the announcement of the investment and operational de-tails for their operations in Gujarat.

Earlier, the company had said a wholly owned subsidiary of Japan's Suzuki Motor Corp would set up the proposed plant in Gujarat that would solely make vehicles for the Indian carmaker.

Maruti has also indicated that the price at which it will acquire cars from the Suzuki subsidiary will cover the direct cost of production. But since the proposed company will be an unlisted entity, one may never get to know the actual cost of production or the cost efficiencies of such an entity.

Secondly, Maruti will end up making only selling/distribution margins on these vehicles. Since Maruti's capital invested for the Gujarat plant would only be the cost of the land it acquired, it expects return on capital to be much higher than the 17 per cent it earns now.

But once the Gujarat capacity comes on stream, the utilization ratio between its existing plants and the Gujarat facility would depend on its product plan, and market demand for different cars. This way, the company could end up with less than optimal utilization of capacity at each of its plants.

Third, the resulting jump in cash reserves in future years as a result of this plan, may not lead to investors getting handsome dividends. The company, which currently has cash reserves of about Rs. 7,500 crore, is looking to invest more in research and development and building its marketing network. With the Gujarat plant originally envisaged for exports, Suzuki may also make India its export hub through this move. Cash reserves could be used for furthering the company's international investments.

What Suzuki's Gujarat Plant Means for Maruti?

'Maruti's decision to give the Gujarat plant to Suzuki may not be the proverbial win-win amid concerns about costly imports and pricing'. After Maruti Suzuki announced that the proposed factory in Gujarat would be owned not by it (as was originally planned) but by a fully owned subsidiary of Suzuki Motor Corporation, the company's stock fell over 8 per cent. It did not mean much for the market that the company had announced a healthy 36 per cent growth in profit for the quarter ended December 2013. Analysts and brokers hammered the share because the move was perceived to harm the interests of the small shareholders and raised serious corporate governance issues.

Yet, just a day later and after a long and heated analyst call with the Maruti Suzuki management, the market changed its mind. The Maruti Suzuki share recovered most of the previous day's loss and closed 7.11 per cent up, the stock was an 'out performer' and 'the actual impact of the deal will be known only in 2017–2018 when the plant starts commercial production.'

Cause of Concern? Should Minority Shareholders Worry or Not?

Many experts feel Suzuki is looking to exercise stricter control over its core business of making cars, and that may have prompted it to house the Gujarat factory in the new fully owned subsidiary, Suzuki Motor Gujarat. (Suzuki owns 56.2 per cent of Maruti Suzuki.) This way, it will have greater control over product development.

Under the new arrangement, the new factory will produce cars which will be sold by Maruti Suzuki. The obvious question is, what is the price at which Suzuki Motor Gujarat will sell to Maruti Suzuki? Maruti Suzuki has made it clear that the new company will sell the cars at a cost price and not at a profit, so Suzuki will not make any return on its investment. The price will be determined on an 'arm's length' basis. And the components will be sourced by Maruti Suzuki.

So, there is no way profits will get transferred from widely owned Maruti Suzuki to closely held Suzuki Motor Gujarat. However, there is nothing to stop the new company in the future–when it produces new models–from selling at a profit. Suzuki is going down the same route as many other multinational corporations in India, parking their most profitable business in a 100 per cent subsidiary, with the listed one either housing the less profitable business or operating just as a marketing arm.

Maruti Suzuki chairman R. C. Bhargava says there is another reason why the new arrangement is good for the company's shareholders: its cash reserves of over Rs. 7,500 crores fetch 8–9 per cent return as interest; this income would have come down if the Gujarat factory was funded out of the reserve. On the other hand, Suzuki, which earns less than 1 per cent on its cash reserves of Rs. 25,000 crores in Japan, will enhance its returns.

Costly Imports

Yet, it might not be so simple. Experts say it won't be easy for the new subsidiary to justify the price of imported components it will buy from Suzuki because it intends to sell the cars to Maruti Suzuki at a cost price. 'This is not the case when the components are imported by Maruti Suzuki', says a transfer pricing expert. 'It will be difficult for the subsidiary to justify the price of imported components unless the components are bought by Maruti Suzuki and then given to the subsidiary'. Bhargava says the problem is not unique to the new subsidiary and such transfer-pricing questions are asked even now to Maruti Suzuki when it imports components because these are related-party transactions.

Tax experts say that under the domestic transfer pricing rules, there is no problem in the deal as the only thing which is scrutinized is expenditure and not income. As the new subsidiary will sell the cars at cost price and the profit margin will be booked by Maruti Suzuki on which it will pay taxes, there is no loss of revenue for the government. However, over a period, income may also be included in the domestic transfer pricing rules. In that case, the Gujarat subsidiary will face serious scrutiny as it has to justify why it is not making profits and at what price would it sell the same cars to third parties.?

Another issue is where will the new models be made? Will they be manufactured now in Gujarat, which means Maruti Suzuki—as well as its shareholders—will lose control over its growth plans? There are some other key issues. if the market drops, who will curtail production?: Maruti Suzuki or the 100 per cent subsidiary? Obviously, the decision in such a scenario will be taken not by Maruti Suzuki but by Suzuki. This is yet another decision that is set to slip out of the hands of the Maruti Suzuki shareholders.

Also, the land in Gujarat is on the books of Maruti Suzuki. This poses another question: When it leases the land to Suzuki Gujarat Motor, will the rental be built into the cost of the vehicle or will it be reimbursed to Maruti Suzuki separately? 'If so, Suzuki will have free access to land that is partly owned by the 44 per cent non-promoter shareholders of Maruti Suzuki. Maruti Suzuki says that the lease rentals will not be as high that will increase the cost of the car, something it can ill-afford in an extremely competitive market'.

Also, the question remains whether the cost of production would be cheaper in the 100 per cent subsidiary.? After all, it will have its own legal and human resource team and cannot use the infrastructure of Maruti Suzuki. This will only raise the cost. Maruti Suzuki says it will offer its employees the option to shift to Gujarat.

The Labour Link

Industry watchers say the move may have also been prompted by Suzuki Chairman Osamu Suzuki's growing concern with labour problems in the Manesar-Gurgaon region, where Maruti Suzuki's two factories are located. Frequent and violent strikes have caused the company significant loss of production in the recent past. 'Inculcating the Japanese method of labour management on Manesar has been a disaster. So it is quite tenable that Suzuki wanted Gujarat to have nothing to do with the existing unions and it prefers to deal with the unions directly rather than through the Indian company'.

The new deal has caused observers to debate the real cause of the move. 'The problem is that whenever you have such a structure there is always the suspicion that the price mechanism is not transparent, especially when you know that Suzuki has tried to get greater control and extract more cash for its balance sheet in Japan', says the former executive of Maruti.

In 2004, Suzuki announced a 70/30 venture with Maruti Suzuki to make cars at Manesar. The deal created a furore, and the government threatened to stop investments by the company. Suzuki relented and the structure was overturned. After legal advice, it was found more prudent to merge it into Maruti Suzuki to avoid questions of transparency. However, it was able to create a 70/30 partnership for power trains which was recently merged into Maruti Suzuki.

Suzuki has also been receiving huge amounts as royalty from Maruti Suzuki, which goes to shore up its profit in Japan. Thus, amongst all the companies listed on the Indian stock exchanges, none pays more royalty than Maruti Suzuki. The royalty payment to Suzuki has jumped nearly fivefold from Rs 493.1 crore in 2007–2008 to Rs. 2,450 crore in 2012–2013. Royalty payment accounts for 5.8 per cent of Maruti Suzuki's net sales in 2012–2013, up from a mere 2.8 per cent in 2007–2008. More strikingly, it constitutes a staggering 47 per cent of Suzuki's profit after tax, say analysts. The basic brunt of the unhappiness about Suzuki's plan is that it will allow the Japanese company to divert its India profits from a company it only partly owns to one it wholly owns, which it can then repatriate home (TOI 24 February 2014). At least seven fund houses have raised a red flag over Suzuki's plan to set up a manufacturing facility in Gujarat and asked for a 'rethink', arguing that the move is 'neither fair nor' in the interest of its 56 per cent-owned Indian arm, Maruti Suzuki, and its minority shareholders.

The shareholders in Maruti Suzuki have also complained about royalty payments by the country's largest carmaker to its Japanese parent. 'Complete clarity and transparency on these issues is needed so that further damage to minority shareholders is avoided. MSIL should do everything possible to ensure that this trust is restored and maintained for ever,' the fund houses said in a joint letter to the Maruti Suzuki chairman Mr. R. C. Bhargava.

On 28 January 2014, the company's board had announced a decision to let Suzuki Motor Corporation set up a 100 per cent subsidiary in Gujarat. Maruti Suzuki will source products from this facility, it had said. The decision was thumbed down by investors, with the stock falling 8 per cent (although it has recovered since).

The basic brunt of the unhappiness about Suzuki's plan is that it will allow the Japanese company to divert its India profits from a company it only partly owns to one it wholly owns, which it can then repatriate home. It was Maruti Suzuki which was originally supposed to set up the plant.

Case Questions

1. What in your opinion are the short-term and long-term issues of this case? What according to you is the long-term strategy of Suzuki

Motors in separating operational controls from Maruti Suzuki to Suzuki Motors in the Gujarat plant?

2. What are the consequences or fallout of this proposal on the IR situations at Manesar & Gurgaon plants—in case of transfer of Employees to the new plant and the reduced stake in the Gujarat Plant might affect prospects of wage revisions negotiations—and productivity concerns?

12

Nokia Manufacturing Unit Knocked Out of India

A Case Study on Issues Involved in the Exit of Nokia from India

Learning Objectives

Many foreign large size companies desirous of establishing their new manufacturing units in India especially lured by the economic and manpower-related incentives by state governments end up getting into serious operational issues including noncooperation and nonfulfillment of earlier promises by the administrative machinery in local bodies.

Many companies including auto majors like GM, Ford, Fiat Chrysler, have had their portion of troubles once having committed to investments and employment guarantees to the local youth after leaving to defend themselves in the smooth running of their ventures.

Nokia even though it was one of the early entrants in Indian mobile manufacturing could never come out of the niggling issues at times due mainly to political interventions and vested interests instigating the labour force to create trouble by the stoppage of operations asking for out of turn wage benefits and adversely affecting managements plans to increase production and revenues. This is one of the common ailments in hurting the ease of doing business in emerging economies like India.

This case study explains the way to evaluate long-term benefits of Investments along with the ability to effectively tackle the local sociopolitical issues, which could work out in detrimental issues leading to inoperable business situations.

Indian Business Case Studies. Varsha Parab, Ramesh Mahadik, and Diksha Tripathi, Oxford University Press.
© ASM Group of Institutes, Pune, India 2022. DOI: 10.1093/oso/9780192869432.003.0012

Synopsis

Once a showpiece of foreign investment, the factory at Sriperumbudur, about 45 km from Chennai, now looks like a ghost entity. For the around 30,000 workers, 31 October 2014 will forever be Black Friday as Nokia officially shutdowns its plant in the state, nine years after it entered India. Nokia's closure will be the first major wind up by a multinational after the Narendra Modi government took charge in May. Established in 2006 over a 200-acre site, Nokia wheeled out the 'Made for India' 1100 model and then slowly ramped up production to make Chennai its single largest unit for handsets globally. Nokia and its suppliers had invested over Rs 1,800 crore in their facilities.

Nokia started operations at Sriperumbudur plant near here–the second-biggest facility by any global firm—in 2006 after Korean auto major Hyundai's came up with its plant in the late 1990s.

After inking the agreement with the Tamil Nadu government in 2004, Nokia began operations at the facility. It directly employed 8,000 people and another 25,000 were associated indirectly with the firm when the facility was operating in full swing. The facility was producing some of the basic GSM handsets. It was serving the local market, besides exports. However, its decision to sell off the handset business to Microsoft Corp in a $7.5-billion deal forced it to keep the factory out of the agreement due to a tax dispute with Indian authorities.

Nokia Company

Nokia is a leader in the fields of network infrastructure, location-based technologies, and advanced technologies. Headquartered in Espoo, Finland, and with operations around the world, Nokia invests in the technologies of the future. Nokia have three strong businesses:

1. Nokia Networks, network infrastructure business;
2. HERE, location intelligence business; and
3. Nokia Technologies, which is focused on technology development and intellectual property rights activities.

Through these businesses, it has a global presence, employing around 57,000 people. Nokia is also a major investor in R&D, with investment through the three businesses amounting to more than EUR2.5 billion in 2013.

Until recently, Nokia also was a key participant in the mobile devices market through its Devices & Services business. In September 2013, Nokia announced an agreement with Microsoft whereby it would sell substantially all of its devices and services business to Microsoft. The transaction was completed on 25 April 2014.

Background History of Nokia

Nokia has a long history of successful change and innovation, adapting to shifts in markets and technologies. From its humble beginning with one paper mill, the company has participated in many sectors over time: cables, paper products, tyres, rubber boots, consumer and industrial electronics, plastics, chemicals, telecommunications infrastructure, and more. Most recently, Nokia has been best known for its revolutionary wireless communication technologies, which have connected billions of people through networks and mobile phones.

Nokia's history dates back to 1865, when mining engineer Fredrik Idestam set up his first wood pulp mill at the Tammerkoski Rapids in Southwestern Finland. A few years later, he opened a second mill on the banks of the Nokianvirta river, inspiring him to name his company Nokia Ab in 1871.

In 1967, It took its current form as Nokia Corporation as a result of the merger of Idestam's Nokia AB, Finnish Rubber Works, a manufacturer of rubber boots, tyres, and other rubber products founded in 1898, and Finnish Cable Works Ltd, a manufacturer of telephone and power cables founded in 1912. The new Nokia Corporation had five businesses: rubber, cable, forestry, electronics, and power generation.

Nokia first entered the telecommunications equipment market in 1960 when an electronics department was established at Finnish Cable Works to concentrate on the production of radio-transmission equipment. Regulatory and technological reforms have played a role in our success.

Deregulation of the European telecommunications industries since the late 1980s has stimulated competition and boosted customer demand.

In 1982, when Nokia introduced the first fully digital local telephone exchange in Europe, and in the same year, the world's first car phone for the Nordic Mobile Telephone analogue standard. The technological breakthrough of GSM, which made more efficient use of frequencies and had greater capacity in addition to high-quality sound, was followed by the European resolution in 1987 to adopt GSM as the European digital standard by 1 July 1991. The first GSM call was made with a Nokia phone over the Nokia-built network of a Finnish operator called Radiolinja in 1991, and in the same year, Nokia won contracts to supply GSM networks in other European countries.

In the early 1990s, it made a strategic decision to make telecommunications its core business, with the goal of establishing leadership in every major global market. Basic industry and non-telecommunications operations—including paper, personal computers, rubber, footwear, chemicals, power plant, cable, aluminium, and television businesses—were divested between 1989 and 1996. By 1998, Nokia was the world leader in mobile phones, a position it enjoyed for more than a decade.

In 2006, Nokia, which had already been investing in its mapping capabilities for many years, acquired Gate5, a mapping software specialist, and then in 2008 NAVTEQ, the US-based maker of digital mapping and navigational software. Today, Nokia offers leading location services through the HERE business and brand, launched in 2012.

In 2007, Nokia combined its telecoms infrastructure operations with those of Siemens to form a joint venture named Nokia Siemens Networks. NSN has become a leading global provider of telecommunications infrastructure, with a focus on offering innovative mobile broadband technology and services.

In 2011, Nokia joined forces with Microsoft to strengthen its position in the highly competitive smartphone market. Nokia adopted the Windows Phone operating system for smart devices and through their strategic partnership Nokia and Microsoft set about establishing an alternative ecosystem to rival iOS and Android. In 2011, Nokia also started to make a number of changes to its operations and company culture that would, in the course of the next two years, lead to shortened product development times, improved product quality, and better responsiveness to market demand.

In 2013, Nokia moved to reinvent itself with two transformative transactions. The first was the purchase of Siemens' stake in NSN, which was nearing the end of a deep restructuring and remarkable transformation. The second was the announcement of the sale of substantially all of Nokia's devices and services business to Microsoft. The Microsoft transaction was originally announced on 3 September 2013 and was completed on 25 April 2014.

Following the closing of the transaction, Nokia announced its new vision and strategy, building on its three strong businesses: Nokia Networks, HERE, and Nokia Technologies.

History of Nokia Operations in India

1 December 2004

Nokia announces its decision to set up a plant in India. Till then, it used to import all handsets sold in India from China.

6 April 2005

Nokia signs MoU with Tamil Nadu to set up the plant in Sriperumbudur Special Economic Zone (SEZ). It invited seven of its ecosystem partners to invest. Nokia initially committed to an investment of about $150 million for five years. Its cumulative investment grew up to $300 million.

2 January 2006

Sriperumbudur plant starts commercial production of handsets with 550 people. Nokia first equipment vendor to manufacture both mobile devices and network infrastructure equipment in India.

11 March 2006

Sriperumbudur facility was inaugurated by Finland's Prime Minister. Factory starts with low and mid-range GSM handsets, which include the Nokia 1100 model. Jorma Ollila, chairman and CEO also present. Sale crosses one million mark in the same month.

June 2009

Sriperumbudur factory has edged past China as a unit-wise volume producer of Nokia cell phones and becomes Nokia's largest cell phone manufacturing facility in the world.

1 May 2010

Nokia crosses 250 million handset mark and starts exports to North America and Europe.

5 May 2011

Production crosses 500 million handsets, marking a significant milestone for Nokia's manufacturing operations in India and globally. The milestone was achieved in five years of its operations, marking Chennai's ramp-up among the fastest globally.

End of March 2014

The plant's cumulative production was 800 million handsets. Exports worth more than $2 billion a year. Nokia India's overall turnover totalled Rs 151,000 crore between 2005/2006 and 2011/2012.

In its prime days, the Sriperumbudur plant was one of its biggest handset manufacturing facilities, producing over three lakh handsets a day. At its peak, the Nokia factory employed around 8,000 people directly and another 25,000 indirectly.

But ever since its tussle with the income-tax authorities for non-payment of dues of Rs. 21,000-crore to the centre and Rs 2,400-crore to the state and the Microsoft take-over deal of Nokia's handset business, the company has been pruning its workforce. Microsoft made it absolutely clear it was not interested in fighting the tax department in India and hence decided to leave the Chennai plant out of the deal.

Overview

Nokia's Organization Structure

Structure optimized for growth and innovation: Nokia has a simple and clear operational governance model, designed to facilitate innovation and growth. Its three businesses report to the Nokia President and Chief Executive Officer, Rajeev Suri, who has full accountability for the performance of the company. HERE and Nokia Technologies each have a single leader reporting to him. To ensure efficiency and simplicity, Mr. Suri assumes direct control of the Nokia Networks business and the key Nokia Networks leaders report to him.

The primary operative decision-making body for the company is the Nokia Group Leadership Team. The Group Leadership Team is responsible for Group level matters, including the company strategy and overall business portfolio.

Go, Get Nokia

It was all very different on 1 December 2004 when Nokia first announced its decision to set up a plant in India. Till then, it used to import all handsets sold in India from China. 'India was doing about a million phones a month at the time', says a former Nokia executive who does not want to be named. 'Nokia wondered how it could make this a six to seven million a month market. The answer was local manufacturing'. An Indian facility meant lower logistics costs, less time to hit the market, more flexibility. No longer would executives have to get in touch with the China factories for small design changes, which took nearly three weeks to be executed and products shipped. When Nokia revealed it was scouting for a manufacturing destination in India, many state governments—Haryana, Andhra Pradesh, Uttarakhand, Karnataka, and Maharashtra, along with Tamil Nadu—competed to woo it.

In 2004, when Nokia first announced that it was scouting for a manufacturing plant in India, Tamil Nadu moved the fastest and won the race. Chief Minister J. Jayalalithaa saw the news clippings and is said to have commanded her babus: 'Go, get Nokia'. Within two days of Nokia's announcement, Tamil Nadu officials were in Delhi, making a presentation before its executives.

Sure, Tamil Nadu's alacrity was not the only reason it won. Sabyasachi Patra, who handled Nokia India's relations with the government between 2005 and 2011, explains why Sriperumbudur was finally chosen. 'Quick access to an international airport was an important condition since phones are low value, high volume products', he says. 'Chennai airport was only 33 km away'.

Uttarakhand and Andhra Pradesh promised to build international airports, but no one in Nokia believed either would be able to do so quickly. (Hyderabad did not have its new airport then; that happened only in 2008.) Maharashtra lost out because of traffic congestion in Mumbai and Karnataka, due to Bangalore's poor infrastructure.

But Patra acknowledges the Tamil Nadu bureaucrats' role. 'They made a good presentation', he says. 'That kind of dialogue was not happening elsewhere'. Just what kind? One of the bureaucrats involved in the discussions throws some light. 'We understand the mind of investors', he says. 'Never say "No problem" to them. That sort of smugness plants doubts'. It also helped that the leading political parties of the state united to welcome Nokia.

'Nokia signed a memorandum of understanding with the Tamil Nadu government on 6 April 2005, to set up the plant in the Sriperumbudur SEZ. It invited seven of its ecosystem partners to invest. Production started in 2006'.

Tax Tussle

January 8, 2013: Income Tax Department inspects the Chennai factory.

March 21, 2013: IT Department issues Rs. 2080 crores tax demand, later rectifies to Rs. 2,649 crores on Nokia. Later matter moved to court.

February 2014: Tamil Nadu sends Rs. 2,400 crores sales tax notice.

April 2014: Nokia completes the sale of devices and services business to Microsoft globally, excluding Chennai factory, which was frozen by IT Department. Company announces VRS to employees.

October 6, 2014: Company says that from 1 November 2014, it will suspend operations at Sriperumbudur as Microsoft is ending its sourcing agreement with Nokia.

In a separate tax case, the Supreme Court had ordered Nokia India on 14 March 2015 to give a Rs. 3,500 crores guarantee before it transfers the plant to Microsoft. As a consequence, Nokia entered into a transitional services agreement with Microsoft to address their immediate production needs and keep the factory operational. 'Unfortunately, the continuing asset freeze imposed by the tax department prevented Nokia from exploring potential opportunities for the transfer of the factory to a successor to support the long-term viability of the established, fully functional electronics manufacturing ecosystem'.

What Triggered to Shutdown

The mothballed Sriperumbudur plant of Nokia, once the world's single largest mobile phone-making unit, may be sold in parts. The Finnish company has appointed Hilco, a global leader in handling distressed investment and assets, to take over the machinery and hard utilities. Hilco officials undertook a due diligence at the factory.

Nokia suspended production at the facility from 1 November. 'They did a complete assessment of the plant and its machinery', sources said. While the value of machinery lying idle inside the plant is not known, sources said that it could be worth close to 54 million euro, including hard utilities like continuous process unit, generators, capacitors, chilling plant, and others. 'The decision to sell the plant in parts was taken by Nokia as take over the plant by a buyer appears remote due to obsolete machinery and technology'.

'Today, nobody makes Nokia phones and therefore the scope for someone to buy the plant appears remote', sources said. The factory, assets of which were frozen by the tax authorities, will move to Central Board of Direct Taxes as Nokia had only an operating license after the tahsildar of Kancheepuram attached it due to non-payment of taxes, as ordered by CBDT. For any transactions at the plant, the courts must defreeze the assets.

In a global transaction, Nokia announced its sale of the handset business, including its Sriperumbudur plant, to Microsoft for 5.4 billion euro last year. The deal deadline of 31 March was extended to April 2014. Several cases and tax disputes surfaced after the deal with Microsoft was announced, and the Sriperumbudur plant was left out of the deal. Nokia ran the plant as a contract manufacturer for Microsoft for one year.

Tax authorities say Nokia violated several tax laws, including transfer pricing laws and permanent establishment liability, which if proven, will result in a tax charge in excess of Rs. 21,000 crore on the Finnish company. 'As of now, the tax authorities have issued demands for Rs 3,080 crore. Of this, Nokia was directed to pay Rs 500 crore by the Delhi high court which the company has paid', sources said. With Nokia shutting down the plant, its key component supplier Foxconn too has announced the suspension of production from 24 December.

Nokia's decision to suspend production in India left many wondering what triggered the move, as the company had earlier said its factory in Sriperumbudur was among its most productive globally. While the tax holiday for the factory coming to an end might be a factor, many say the business model of Microsoft (which acquired Nokia's handset division last year), as well as freebies offered by the Vietnamese government, might also have played a role.

The US firm said it would focus on the mass Smartphone market. 'There is no future if you don't have share. We will build scale and share. We will unlock more products in the $100-200 price range to address the mass market', Chakrapani Gollapali, country general manager (consumer channels group) at Microsoft Corporation India, had said earlier.

The company's 'affordable' smartphones would hit the market in three-four months, he added. Currently, the company has one product in this category—the Nokia Lumia 520.

HR Issues at Nokia

Plant Shut Down

The plant's shutdown has rendered over 8,000 workers jobless. While both DMK and AIDMK welcomed Nokia with a red carpet when it decided to set up shop in Sriperumbudur, both political parties have done little except stage protests to oppose Nokia's decision to suspend production.

Nokia shuts the Chennai factory (Black Friday for workers). Workers fret over future, over 30,000 people were affected. With Nokia deciding to suspend operations, trade unions as well as political parties have asked the government to take over the factory to protect the livelihood of thousands of workers.

A Soundararajan, general secretary of Centre of Trade Unions (CITU) and a sitting member of the Tamil Nadu Legislative Assembly, said the CITU has asked the state and central governments to take over the factory.

Nokia India Employees Union, which claims to have the backing of workers at the factory, is backed by CITU. Earlier, in order to protect the interests of workers at Neyveli Lignite Corporation, a central government-run company, the Tamil Nadu government had come forward to acquire a five per cent stake in the company, which the central government was planning to dilute to outsiders.

Similarly, the state government or the central should take over the Sriperumbudur factory, taking thousands of Nokia workers' livelihoods into consideration, Soundararajan said. He said the factory could manufacture mobile phones, laptops, and set-up boxes. So, if the government can convince customers such as Microsoft and others, orders will start flowing to the factory, he noted.

The major reason given by Nokia for suspending operations at the Sriperumbudur plant is a lack of orders, especially after Microsoft decided to stop sourcing from the plant. With the month-long voluntary retirement scheme (VRS) announced by Nokia India coming to an end on Wednesday, 15 May 2014, 5,000 employees of the mobile handset facility in Sriperumbudur near here have opted for it. Another 400 are expected to opt for VRS. This could be one of the largest VRS offered by any company in India in recent times, said sources.

The factory directly employs 6,700. A little over 60 per cent are women.

Nokia India said, 'While we set no target for the VRS in terms of employees, 5,000 have opted for it.' Workers who had not opted for VRS asked, 'With the balance 1,700 workers, how will the factory be run?' The company said, 'Nokia intends to respect commitments under the services contract'. Workers said many had queued at the office to opt for VRS on Wednesday. The union has demanded a withdrawal of VRS.

On those opting for VRS, sources said workers in the facility for five years or more (some have been for eight) would get the compensation that would include a 15-month salary (each year of experience would be three months). Those with less than five years would be compensated on a similar basis. A worker would get Rs. 1 lakh each as compensation and double the daily salary for the earned leave surrendered. To support those that have taken up VRS, the company has introduced a bridge initiative. It is offering banking consultancy services and employment outlook training. It is introducing initiatives under the bridge.

These include working with experts to identify new employment areas, developing suitable training and skilling employees, conducting awareness sessions to share information on 30 skill development modules and employment outlook training schemes across sectors. The company said, 'The training programmes will be held over a period at 40 locations in Tamil Nadu, including Chennai'. It would certify employees on the skills learnt, invite potential employers to facilitate placements and give limited grants to support entrepreneurial or academic ambitions of those who have worked for six years or more.

Around 72 per cent of the Nokia plant's employees were women. Indeed, the job with Nokia transformed the lives of many of the women, most of who were from poor families—young high school pass outs taking up their first jobs. 'We realized the importance of Nokia not only from the narrow angle of employment generation but also through the change it brought about in the employees' lives', Patra says.

There are around 8,000 employees under direct employment in the facility where as around 21,000 are employed indirectly for the company in Sriperumbudur. Meanwhile, sources inform that almost all the over 700 trainees are resigning from the company, accepting the retirement option offered by the company. According to the union sources, the package offered by the company for trainees includes three month gross salary along with Rs. 2 lakhs as compensation. Nokia employees at Sriperumbudur to get a severance package of Rs. 7.5 lakhs each.

A final settlement was reached for over 900 workers still employed at Nokia's phone manufacturing unit in Sriperumbudur on Thursday, a day before the official closure of the plant. The deal arrived at gives the staff a sum slightly higher than the amount of Rs 6 lakh announced through a VRS.

'The plant has been operating at Sriperumbudur near Chennai since 2005 and enjoying several benefits offered by the state government since then. However, without intimating the labourers, the state or central government, the company was sold to Microsoft'.

Case Questions

1. Did politicians cock a snook at Nokia staff? Why job security of about 30,000 employees (directly and indirectly employed) was simply not taken care of by central and state governments?

2. Why could Nokia not look at the possibilities of taking the case to international courts?

3. Why could Nokia Tamil Nadu factory not be saved, though the government had the option of running under public–private partnership?

4. The rise and fall of Nokia's Sriperumbudur plant raise larger questions about India's attractiveness—or otherwise—as a manufacturing destination.

5. Given Nokia's experience, why would anyone set up an electronics plant in India when China, Taiwan, and some East European countries are established destinations?

13

When the Going Got Tough—The Tough Ones Gave Up?

A Case Study of Unexpected Product Failures of Established Brands Like the Tatas

Learning Objectives

This is a case study on complex issues of failure of products otherwise expected to be trendsetters and game changers in the marketplace.

In spite of the fact that products like Tatas Nano car having received accolades and appreciations from global experts in the small car segment of the auto industry, considering Tatas Nano as one with the groundbreaking product feasibility criteria expected to revolutionize the concept of the world's first smallest passenger car coming from a highly reputed and respected Tata Motors stable with its creator Mr. Ratan Tata's highly regarded and popular personality as strong tag and brand image. It had to forcefully fall, on its face flat, and finished within less than 2–3 years of its launch.

What went wrong was that within a few years of its launch, the Tatas Nano had to be withdrawn from the market and a house like Tatas who do not succumb to challenges ever, had to meekly accept the market response of one of the utter failure of a mystic Product Nano unlike any other product launch by any other Tata group in the history so far.

One normally expected even in spite of initial reactions, Tatas would hit back with surprising corrective and moderation steps and relaunch Nano back with a bang, but that did not happen giving a jolt to the confidence level of multi-million fans of the Tatas.

Indian Business Case Studies. Varsha Parab, Ramesh Mahadik, and Diksha Tripathi, Oxford University Press.
© ASM Group of Institutes, Pune, India 2022. DOI: 10.1093/oso/9780192869432.003.0013

There are similar situations faced by other products and brands of failures against expected recoveries. But none can be compared to the Regret felt by the Tata Nano failure.

This case study gives glimpses of such situations making the students of new product launch and product branding and [positioning strategy a food for thought to understand the possibility of such situations leading to helpless plight of the tougher ones as well.

Synopsis

This case is about classic examples of failures in new product launch and rebranding of products. The case in the content and the background has the failure of Tata Nano car, which even today is like a bad dream severely affecting and shaking the confidence in an industry stalwart like Ratan Tata and his impeccable track record of success stories as a great entrepreneur and a technocrat.

Case Details

In the early 1950s, Marlboro had a problem. Famous for selling 'Mild as May' women's cigarettes since 1924, the brand was struggling with low sales because of lung cancer concerns among this audience set. It was a limited success, acquiring around 1 per cent market share. Men liked smoking filtered cigarettes because they perceived them to be safer, but they didn't want to touch a woman's brand.

Consider this: even the filter had a printed red band around it to hide lipstick stains.

This was when the forces behind Marlboro decided the time for repositioning the brand had come. The result? The 'Marlboro Man' captured everything Marlboro now wished to stand for: manliness. It worked: Marlboro went on to become a power brand.

Repositioning could just be the right cure for an ailing brand that has stuck to a said formula. Motives could vary from declining sales, to the current target audience no longer being relevant. In some cases, the product itself could have evolved significantly, competition could have magnified, or customers could find your brand 'outdated'–all reasons that scream for a repositioning exercise.

With that in mind, let's look at two brands closer home that have opted for makeovers in some sense. The first is Tata Nano, Tata Motors' 'people's car' launched in 2009. Chairman Emeritus of the Tata group, Nano's creator Ratan Tata recently admitted that positioning the brand Nano as the cheapest car was a big mistake. And he wouldn't be wrong—Nano was supposed to be a revolutionary concept, an engineering marvel, and a game changer.

It failed to take off despite the Tata brand goodwill. Initial engine mishaps, quality issues, and most of all, a wrong communication plank ensured the brand was written off from the consideration set of even the 'value' buyer.

The Brand Now Wishes to Target the Youth

The second brand on our list is Cadbury Gems, the chocolate brand that embodies everything child-like, right from its bright and colourful button-shaped chocolate balls, to its packaging and communication. In 2012, the brand underwent a repositioning–it changed tack to target adults, particularly the tweens and teenagers, telling them they are never too old to love Gems (the 'Raho umarless' campaign).

Eyebrow-raising, considering how much Gems is entrenched in consumer minds as a kid's product. Experts point out this could be a result of stagnating sales or possibly, an attempt to go down the same path as predecessor Dairy Milk, which started targeting adults in the 1990s. Together, the two brands offer a world of insight into the concept of repositioning. When is it a good time to rethink what your brand stands for? Can pricing have a bearing on the fate of a positioning strategy? And most importantly—are you doing it for the right reasons, and in the right way?

First, let's take the Nano. Positioning it as a 'cheap' product means it was immediately equated with bad quality in the minds of the potential buyers. Its sales have been dipping steadily. In a slowing economy, with high-interest rates and fuel prices, Nano sales volumes slipped to below 1,000 units in April 2013. 'The Indian consumer is an aspirational one, and even a two-wheeler owner looking to upgrade will not want a cheap car', says Amit Kaushik, principal analyst. The brand is planning a turn-around exercise with new additions such as power steering, fancy wheel covers, remote keyless entry, twin glove boxes, a music system, and a diesel variant to target the youth in a 'smart city car' avatar. 'It is imperative that we clearly articulate the value that a brand like Nano brings at a certain price point, as opposed to being cheap because there has been a misconception around the price-tag'.

'The new Nano is aimed at a younger, aspiring consumer class and good value does not mean cheap', says a Tata Motors spokesperson.

Its communication, which released recently, 'Celebrating awesomeness', is proof to this effect—a supposed move from 'cheap' to 'decent'. 'Targeting the youth might be the other extreme... the young, bike zone'.

'This is a 360-degree switch and not sure it will work. Frankly, there seems to be confusion on what to do with the product. 'Also, with diesel prices shooting up, a diesel variant may not be able to save the day', he says.

Clearly, Nano has a lot of work to do. The brand has, in a sense, compromised the prestige value of owning a car (a matter of great pride in India) in the eyes of consumers, say some industry watchers. While it is commendable that Tata Motors has decided to extricate the Nano from its earlier association with 'cheap', it is a matter of debate if targeting the youth—particularly entry-level car owners or bike owners—is the right answer.

Let's understand the category Nano wishes to compete in. The car currently falls in the ultra low cost or the sub-A segment. So Nano will probably target the A segment (with cars like Alto falling under it). Competing with bikes for attention may be an even tougher job to do, even if it is an affordable upgrade. This would have probably worked better in mature markets like Europe and the US, where bikes are a luxury and an affordable car positioned on the price plank could work well. The concept of commuter bikes, after all, is very South Asian.

'It is easier to change a brand's positioning when it moves from one country to another', hinting that the Nano probably ought to look beyond India for success now.

So clearly, price can be a strong positioning plank in some markets, but ironically, in price-sensitive India, pricing alone can't carry the baton. Coca-Cola, for instance, gave up the Rs 5 price positioning after sometime. 'Price can't be a long-term positioning premise in India. Else you land up with a Nano.'

Many liquor brands have been successful though, just by pricing their brands higher than their competitors, like Absolut and Grey Goose. But as branding experts put it, to make this strategy work, your brand needs to be the first to occupy the high-price position.

Generally, brands tend to shut up on the communication front if the product has become more expensive. If it has gotten cheaper, the brand might appear as a 'discounted', bargain one—not always an alluring bet in aspirational categories like cars. So playing with the price is like playing with fire—one has to be well equipped to carry the act through.

Are the Right Reasons at Play?

The longevity of a brand's presence matters when it comes to positioning. It is difficult to change the perceptions of brands that have been around for a long time. In the US, Coca-Cola is known as 'The real thing'. Yet the advertising for the past few years has focused on 'Open happiness. The general belief is that most people consider Cola-Cola to be the real thing and few people identify it with happiness. On the other hand, recently launched brands don't have such strong identities, so it is relatively easier to change them.

This brings us to Cadbury Gems, a brand that has been around for decades, symbolizing childhood, fun, 'masti' and excitement. Sometime ago, Gems launched its Panda commercial to get kids excited about the brand all over again, and even launched a new packaging in a ball-like shape, called Gems Surprise, which included little Pandas as collectibles. So it came as a surprise when the brand started targeting adults as well with 'Raho Umarless' last year. Siddhartha Mukherjee, executive director, chocolate category and media, Cadbury India, says, 'Gems has always been a favourite offering among kids. The new communication says that you never really outgrow the fun that this brand can provide'.

Fair enough, and the move is reminiscent of Cadbury's strategy to grow the pie and target the adult segment in the 1990s with Dairy Milk. What is perhaps different is that Dairy Milk did it when the whole market was about kids' chocolate, so it was a bold step on its part. The market has changed since, and it maturely divided into chocolates for kids and adults.

'Why should a brand take away the biggest joy a kid has, namely Gems?'. 'Even if the brand's sales are stagnating, Gems should probably have refreshed its communication and targeted today's restless kid'.

If a brand undergoes an audience shift, it has taken a conscious call that its current strategy is not working for its existing audience. 'But in Gems' case, it is a dangerous thing to do, as it is working here! It shouldn't be about widening the target group, it should be about using the right insight for today's child'.

Interestingly, Gems hasn't changed as a product when it talks of including adults. Can repositioning be relevant in such cases, where there may not be something new to say? It is a misplaced and outdated notion that a brand can't be repositioned if the product offering hasn't been suitably modified.

Brands and consumers have a complex relationship, like every relationship, this relationship gets affected involuntarily over time. It is important to acknowledge this change. 'What is most important from a brand custodian's point of view, or should be, is to keep the relationship interesting. If that means a repositioning exercise, it means a repositioning exercise'.

The Lessons to Be Learnt

Nano, in its class, is drawing comparisons with the Volkswagen Beetle, which was originally launched in 1950 as a small, reliable, no-nonsense vehicle for those who wanted a car that was economical to own and run. But the price was never mentioned in the advertising.

Thanks to the car's iconic shape and the fact that it was enthusiastically adopted by the generation belonging to the 1960s counter-culture in the US, it also became a symbol of 'flower-power', a statement against the excesses of the big, flashy gas-guzzlers of that time.

Positioning the Nano as a youth vehicle doesn't change its perception as a cheap car. Actually, it deepens those perceptions by suggesting that young people can't afford something better Tatas should do two things.

Figure out a positive positioning for its Nano brand and then change the brand name to heighten those positive perceptions.

That said, a repositioning exercise might not even have much to do with a brand at times; the market may have changed, for one.

Consider smartphones. BlackBerry with its keypad was once a dominant smartphone brand. But the introduction of the iPhone changed consumer perceptions and everybody wanted a touchscreen smartphone.

So BlackBerry introduced a slew of touchscreen smartphones that failed to take off because the perception of the brand (the keypad) was so strong. What BlackBerry could have done, according to analysts, is introduce a touchscreen smartphone with a new brand name.

The lesson: Perhaps a brand shouldn't try to change strongly held perceptions. And for brands like Nano and Gems, it is currently a wait-and-watch game.

Case Questions

1. When is the ideal time for a brand to change/tweak its core positioning?

2. In the case of the car from Tata Motors, Nano, Ratan Tata was recently quoted saying that positioning of the Nano as the 'cheapest car' was a big mistake. Do you agree? Does such positioning make transition tricky?

3. Are there examples of brands that have climbed up the ladder by repositioning on the pricing premise?

14

The 'Prestigious' Growth

A Case Study in Strategic Marketing
Prestige Pressure Cookers

Learning Objectives

The students of strategic management and marketing need to understand concepts on competitive advantage strategies based on cost and differentiation as the main focus.

These concepts need to be clarified and consolidated through Case Studies in strategic marketing. This case study on highly popular brands like Prestige Pressure Cookers from the TTK group known for its technology and product marketing capabilities as the way Prestige brand is constantly evolving itself through marginal changes in product positioning including product modifications to suit customers' preferences.

Synopsis

This case is about the challenges faced by the TTKs Prestige brand of kitchen equipment, listing down the journey of Prestige Sofar and the periodical market survey and rebranding strategy as adopted by TTK to sustain the market and grow on its revenues.

Case Details

On 29 June 2010, while addressing shareholders at TTK Ltd's 54th annual general meeting in Hosur, the chairman of TTK, Mr. Jagannathan, made an interesting detour. Not so long, he had told the shareholders, that the

Indian Business Case Studies. Varsha Parab, Ramesh Mahadik, and Diksha Tripathi, Oxford University Press.
© ASM Group of Institutes, Pune, India 2022. DOI: 10.1093/oso/9780192869432.003.0014

company was in the grip of a crisis. The combination of high excise and sales taxes had punched a hole in its pocket, and exports had taken a hit after the 9/11 terrorist attacks on the United States.

The low point was reached in 2002–2003: Sales had slumped to Rs. 113 crores, there was an operating loss of Rs. 17 crores in the company's books and the debt burden had mounted to Rs. 80 crores. With quite renewed pride, Jagannathan read out the numbers for 2009–2010: Turnover of Rs. 516 crores, operating income of Rs. 76 crores and free cash balances of Rs. 30 crores, in spite of capital expenditure of Rs. 40 crores.

The dip in the fortunes in the previous years had actually prompted a significant course correction for the company. TTK Prestige at that time had a single product in its portfolio, pressure cookers. Ten per cent excise-duty meant that the unorganized sector had a field day. Indeed, local price-sensitive brands that functioned under the radar screen of the excise collectors enjoyed a market share in excess of 50 per cent in the Rs. 900 crores market. And TTK Prestige was heavily dependent on the southern markets for sales, though it had some presence in the west. Its visibility was nominal in the north and the east. There was an urgent need to guard itself against these risks.

The question was, in which direction should it expand? Its flagship brand 'Prestige' had over the years built strong equity amongst women in the kitchen. This was a strength TTK prestige could leverage. Thus, it was decided to grow into a kitchen equipment sector. Some bit of the diversification plan was also driven by market research, some by gut-feel and some by simple observation. Jagannathan had personally visited a small village with a population of 5,000 and found that nobody had a pressure cooker. That was very surprising.

What caught his attention was an indication of the business potential which lay unexploited over the years. The company had launched stoves, mixers, grinders, grills, coffee makers, toasters, and even chimneys and modular kitchens. TTK 'Prestige' was visible only in 228 'Prestige' Smart Kitchen outlets in 136 towns to showcase its range of products.

Kitchenware in India has always been sold through multi-brand outlets. As a result, a brand offer with ten products provided a higher profit margin to the retailers to gain a prime slot on the display window. Aware of this fact may not be of interest to the company, TTK had opted for its own flagship stores. In addition to 'Prestige Smart Kitchen', the company also has its 'Prestige Kitchen Boutiques' for modular kitchens. It had even set up 'Prestige Life Style' stores for top-end products, but the initiative has been withdrawn. Ever since the exclusive Prestige Smart Kitchen stores came up, TTK Prestige executives claim that the sales picked up in the multi-brand outlets as well.

The expansion in the product portfolio and retail network was accomplished by outsourcing. Production capacity increase, it was felt, may derail the company's plans. The other reason is that many kitchenware items were reserved for production in the small-scale sector, and outsourcing was a convenient way to overcome this hurdle for a large company like TTK. 'I blame my grandfather (T. T. Krishnamachari who was the erstwhile Finance Minister of India) for the present condition of Indian industry. The policy of reservation did not allow anybody to scale up. Meanwhile look where China's industrial sector has reached today', says Mr. Jagannathan.

So, what has been the result on the ground? Pressure cooker, which contributed the bulk, TTK 'Prestige' sales, now accounts for 46 per cent, Kitchen appliances contribute only 20 per cent to the overall sales, non-stick cookware 17 per cent, and gas stoves 12 per cent, and the rest 5 per cent modular kitchens. Its share in the kitchen appliances market is small, less than 10 per cent. But the company claims that this market is growing faster (30 per cent per annum) than the total market (10 to 15 per cent), and the size of this share in the pie is on the rise.

This is not to say that TTK has put the pressure cooker business on the backburner. In 2005, after some hectic lobbying by the industry, the government reduced the excise tax on pressure cookers from 10 per cent to nil. This was a huge plus for companies like TTK Prestige. As a result, the share of the local unorganized brand in the market came down to about a third. Of the other two-thirds, TTK Prestige lords it over half.

Mr. Jagannathan is perhaps aware that it will not be easy for him to raise his market share from here; that's why the headway into kitchen appliances market makes sense. Also, the technology used in pressure cooker is elementary and it can be mastered by anybody also, there are no entry barriers. TTK Prestige has tried to create some differentiation through innovations in design. Some time back, for instance, it launched the 'Apple' range of pressure cookers which were shaped like an apple. It has launched pressure cookers with a long-lasting coating and one that is built like a Handi, the traditional North-Indian cooking vessel.

However, the market observers feel that TTK Prestige hasn't created enough technological barriers in the new areas it has entered 'Many other who entered the business had to exit as they could not meet consumer demands and were unable to provide high quality products'. The observers also caution against the use of imported products, especially from low-cost producers in China, because of quality problems.

Others feel Prestige, being a hard-core pressure cooker brand, does not lend itself to an extension to appliances. 'Prestige's association with pressure cooker makes it a little difficult to have an impact in kitchen appliances' says Mr. Milagrow (Business & Knowledge Solution founder) and former Philips chief executive, Rajeev Agarwal says 'People will be a little skeptical of its appliances as it is better known for its pressure cookers and non-stick cookware. It will have to ensure quality and features to attract the consumers'.

Mr. Jagannathan, on his part, is convinced that the company is on the right track, though he knows that there are certain issues that need to be sorted out; one such issue is how to tackle the rural markets? With increased farm income, the demand for pressure cookers and even kitchen appliances is on the rise. These markets, it so happens, have always been serviced by local players and national brands do not have much of a presence.

TTK Prestige has developed a new business model involving non-government organizations (NGOs) and self-help groups to sell pressure cookers in rural India. The initial investment will be from the company, while the management will be provided by the NGOs. The company hopes to boost its revenue from the rural market with this model in place.

The other bit of the problem was the expansion to the Northern part of India. TTK Prestige had in 1997 set up a factory in Uttarakhand for inner-lid pressure cookers. The factory benefits from the tax sops on offer, on excise as well as corporation tax. The company has decided to expand this factory to make kitchen appliances like mixers and grinders, gas stoves, and induction cooktops, etc. But it will need to look at its products strategy for the North carefully. Unlike the South, meal preparation in the North does not require heavy grinding and blending; as a result, the food processor market there is different from the southern states.

What TTK Prestige seems to be banking on, is its additional expenditure on sales promotion—this year 2016, the company has a budget of Rs. 50 crores. With our tagline 'Are you ready for a smarter kitchen'?, we have always aimed at making the loudest noise in the kitchen appliance market', says TTK Prestige executive vice-president (marketing), Chandru Kalra.

It is also clear that the company will focus on the domestic market. It has after all got singled out badly in markets overseas. Exports were a huge focus for TTK Prestige in the 1990s and the early years of the current decade. It had started a new brand called 'Mantra' for the US market and even set up a subsidiary there, called 'Mantra Inc', to develop the market. A team of 25 salesmen was taken on board and soon, several retailers were selling Mantra pressure cookers. Then came the bankruptcies and other scandals, etc.

We decided to withdraw from the market, says Jagannathan. At the moment, only Sears and K-Mart sell its wares. One of TTKs' retailers hasn't paid the company for 300,000 pieces, while another one rejected a consignment of 400,000 pieces. Wal-Mart, the biggest retailer, is out of bounds because it wants deliveries within 24 hours. Wiser now, Jagannathan says, 'When the Indian market is doing so well, we are not very keen on exports'.

Case Questions

1. Do you see the marketing strategy of The TTK group as a long-term 'growth' strategy? With the current strategy in place, how much do you project would be the revenue growth and market share increase in the next five years?

2. Comment on the product mix and the outsourcing strategy of TTK. Do you wish to suggest any changes which would ensure growth in market share?

3. In today's globalized market, is the 'India only' strategy appropriate in the long-term competitive advantage position for TTK?

4. Suggest a long-term product versus market portfolio analysis for TTK, highlighting the star performers and the cash cows by developing a BCG matrix for TTK.

15

Nestle Maggi-Noodles Banned in India

Learning Objectives

Effect of conflicting market forces at times appearing to be vindictive on purpose does shake the confidence even of global giants who basically have invested to capture greener pastures of emerging markets by launching their proven products more carefully in the fast-food category, which is susceptible to turbulent headwinds in case of certain negligence to quality issues of direct in gradients in the product considered harmful and hazardous to the consumers' safety and health issues.

Especially during times when even the socio-political climate is pro-indigenization and preference to local manufacturers, one needs to be extra careful in avoiding direct conflicts with a sense of forbearance from long-term business sustainability considerations. It is interesting to see as how carefully Nestle handled the issues involved for the full resurrection of its market positioning in fast food markets.

Synopsis

Maggi seems to be just that perfect quick-snack between meals and is so easy to make the kids sometimes make it alone. At the end of May 2015, India's Food safety administration (FDA) ordered Nestle India to recall its popular Maggi noodles after tests showed that the product contained high levels of lead and MSG. This was suspected to be a vindictive action on another wise globally accepted product basically instigate the consumer of required preference to native brands which aspired to forcefully invade the fast-food market.

Nestle, the makers of Maggie noodles, had to withdraw tons of product stocks from its distribution and sales outlets to basically avoid a direct

Indian Business Case Studies. Varsha Parab, Ramesh Mahadik, and Diksha Tripathi, Oxford University Press.
© ASM Group of Institutes, Pune, India 2022. DOI: 10.1093/oso/9780192869432.003.0015

clash with regulatory authorities and re-establish by immediate corrective steps and repeat lab tests to prove to the authorities that all necessary corrective steps have been taken on priority.

But the dent in customer confidence due to actions by the FAD officials was quite damaging, and it cost Nestle time, money, and patience for re-entry.

Case Details

The company used various social media channels to take care of its image while the media was putting questions on its image.

Initially, the company rejected the accusation that the noodles were unsafe and said on their website and social media accounts that there had been no order to recall any products. A statement on their website said, 'The quality and safety of our products are the top priorities for our company. We have in place strict food safety and quality controls at our Maggi factories. We do not add MSG to Maggi Noodles, and glutamate, if present, may come from naturally occurring sources. We are surprised with the content supposedly found in the sample as we monitor the lead content regularly as a part of the regulatory requirements'.

Nestle continued to keep its customers up to date on the investigation into the safety of Maggi noodles in India. Nestle stated on the official Maggi noodles Facebook page, Twitter, and website that extensive testing revealed no excess lead in Maggi noodles.

Nestle used its Twitter and Facebook accounts to answer customers' questions about the levels of MSG and lead found in their noodles. The company continued to reassure customers that the noodles are safe and that they are a transparent company working closely with authorities in India to resolve the issue.

Nestle recalled all Maggi noodles from India. After reassuring customers that its noodles are safe, the brand did a U-turn and decided to recall Maggi noodles from the shelves. CEO Paul Bulcke said, 'We are working with authorities to clarify the situation and in the meantime Nestle will be withdrawing Maggi noodles from shelves'. Nestle decided to destroy more than $50million worth of Maggi Noodles in India after they were deemed unsafe by regulators.

Even as people back in India are left craving for their favourite instant noodles, Maggi, reports said that the India Research Center of Harvard Business School (HBS) would conduct a case study on the noodles.

The case study discusses what led to the recall of the noodles, which may be completed within a month, which is quite quick compared to the nine months that HBS takes to complete such studies.

Maggi, something that Indians had come to love since it was launched in the early 90s, was taken off the shelves after it was found to have high lead content. And while Maggi has been off the shelves for over two months now, a Bombay High Court order had quashed the ban on Maggi noodles and ordered fresh tests.

However, the government had said the verdict did not alter the grounds on which it had claimed Rs. 640 crore in damages from Nestle for misleading advertisement and unfair trade practices.

The Food Safety and Standards Authority of India (FSSAI) too were still convinced about why the ban was imposed on the instant noodles brand. The regulator maintained that the ban was imposed after thorough tests on the products and had questioned Nestle's extensive disposal of existing Maggi stock.

On behalf of the consumers, the Food and Consumer Affairs Ministry separately filed a Class Action Suit against Nestle India before the National Consumer Disputes Redressed Commission (NCDRC), using a hitherto unused provision in the three-decade-old Consumer Protection Act. In this case, the Centre had claimed damages worth Rs. 640 crores on Nestle.

The Ministry had sought Rs. 284.45 crores in basic damages and further Rs. 355.50 crores in punitive damages, resulting in total damages of Rs. 639.95 crores from the Swiss giant.

Nestle, which had to recall the popular noodles brand after orders from the central food safety regulator FSSAI and food regulators in various states, is the first foreign firm in India to face a class action suit.

With the launch of Maggi noodles, Nestle India Limited (NIL) created an entirely new food category, instant noodles—in the Indian packaged food market. Because of its first-mover advantage, NIL successfully managed to retain its leadership in the instant noodles category even until the early 2000s.

Over the years, NIL extended the Maggi brand to a variety of culinary products like soups, sauces and ketchup, and cooking aids, among others. However, these product extensions were not as successful as the instant noodles. In 2005, NIL started offering a range of new 'healthy' products under the Maggi brand, in a bid to attract health-conscious consumers.

When Maggi was deemed unsafe in India, all eyes were on Nestle to see how they would respond and manage the situation. Nestle defended its product on all social media channels and rejected all claims that its noodles were unsafe. They used the best use of social media to connect the masses. Initially, the websites which were used for the promotion of the product were now being used for maintaining its image.

Maggi India's Twitter account makes an impressive effort to respond to every tweet from customers on this issue with a pre-prepared statement explaining that lead occurs naturally in soil and water. Nestle also explained the science behind the reason for the ban in simple terms so customers could understand.

The scare was a huge blow to the company, which has been selling its Maggi products for over three decades in India with 80% of the country's instant noodle market. However, through smart use of social media during the crisis, the brand limited further damage by reassuring and informing customers to encourage them to continue buying the noodles in the future.

Nestle India is preparing a blueprint for a possible re-launch of the Maggi instant noodles brand. Industry experts and analysts feel the issue of the recall and ban of Maggi noodles in India is likely to be resolved in the next three to six months.

Customer Expectations

Your customers expect you to deliver quality products. If you do not, they will quickly look for alternatives. Quality is critical to satisfying your customers and retaining their loyalty so they continue to buy from you in the future. Quality products make an important contribution to long-term revenue and profitability. They also enable you to charge and maintain higher prices.

Reputation

Quality influences your company's reputation. The growing importance of social media means that customers and prospects can easily share both favourable opinions and criticism of your product quality on forums, product review sites, and social networking sites, such as Facebook and Twitter. A strong reputation for quality can be an important differentiator in markets that are very competitive. Poor quality or a product failure that results in a product recall campaign can create negative publicity and damage your reputation.

Meeting Standards

Accreditation to a recognized quality standard may be essential for dealing with certain customers or complying with legislation. Public sector companies, for example, may insist that their suppliers achieve accreditation with quality standards. If you sell products in regulated markets, such as health care, food, or electrical goods, you must be able to comply with health and safety standards designed to protect consumers. Accredited quality control systems play a crucial role in complying with those standards. Accreditation can also help you win new customers or enter new markets by giving prospects independent confirmation of your company's ability to supply quality products.

Costs

Poor quality increases costs. If you do not have an effective quality control system in place, you may incur the cost of analysing nonconforming goods or services to determine the root causes and retesting products after reworking them. In some cases, you may have to scrap defective products and incur additional production costs to replace them. If defective products reach customers, you will have to pay for returns and replacements and, in serious cases, you could incur legal costs for failure to comply with customer or industry standards.

Case Questions

1. 'Sound quality of the product is the basic foundation for brand-building'. Explain in detail in view of Maggi-Noodles case.

2. What step/action does Nestle India need to take to re-establish its flagship brand (Maggi India) in view of the competition from ITC and Patanjali?

16

The 'Drag-Effect'

A Case Study of Constraints in a Family-Managed Enterprise in a Small-Scale Sector

Learning Objectives

(The case contents are based on a questionnaire survey done by an Indian Team with the objective of developing a live case study on Mexican SMEs.)

Managing business sustainability in family-managed small/medium-sized industries, more so when there is succession by the next generation, tends to become a bit sensitive on account of the sentiments of the earlier generation running strong towards the perpetuation of the promoter's vision, mission, and objectives towards products and markets.

The case explains a similar situation being effectively steered forward in a family-managed business in Mexico.

Synopsis

M/S Villahi Chemicals is a small-scale enterprise dealing in the manufacturing and trading of cleaning chemicals. Hygiene products, tissue papers etc., are required by individual customers as well as for domestic and commercial establishments. This is purely a family (VILLAVICENCIO) managed business established eight years ago in Ensenada in North-Western México. The unit manufactures 50% of its products in-house and 50% of the products are traded from different manufacturers. The total investment is to the tune of $500.000.00 includes machinery and infrastructural facilities.

The unit is closely monitored by the family members; Ms. Yesica Villavicencio, the elder sister, looks after the overall business and is

Indian Business Case Studies. Varsha Parab, Ramesh Mahadik, and Diksha Tripathi, Oxford University Press.
© ASM Group of Institutes, Pune, India 2022. DOI: 10.1093/oso/9780192869432.003.0016

expected to be soon succeeded by her younger brother, Mr. Arturo, who presently is the GM of the setup. One of the major suppliers, M/S Georgia Pacific, is the strategic partner in the business.

The gross turnover of Villahi in the year 2011 was $7,20,000.00 and has grown at an average rate of 15–20% over the previous four to five years. Even though Villahi has major competition from branded products of large-scale manufacturers, it has been able to establish its own market segment through personal follow-up and advertisements through local TV channels, posters, hoardings, and radio media. On its own seal, Villahi has developed a home-grown ERP system to keep a close follow-up with its customer base.

The major concern for the management of Villahi over the previous few years is the very slow pace of strategic decision-making and the increasing competition from the local as well as the neighbouring US manufacturers of chemicals. This situation is further aggravated due to the transition expected at the top management level, which may not have an open-hearted welcome from all the family members. This may impede the business's survival and growth amidst the severity of competition and increasing costs due to older machines and lower productivity at Villahi.

While Mr. Arturo has to take fuller responsibility and drive the options of organizational restructuring including fresh investments in the modernization of older Machines, etc., he is feeling a major drag on his initiative on account of the extremely slow pace of decision-making at crucial times for the business. The organization is gradually slipping into operational paralysis on a strategic approach for a business turnaround and if not shaken up from its slumber, is likely to lose its major markets to its competitors.

On the other hand, the market for cleaning chemicals is growing at a faster pace attracting spurious suppliers from the US markets. It is a real 'catch 22' situation for Villahi and every player in the business to capture as much of market share as is possible.

Case Details

M/S. Villahi & Co—over the previous eight years, has been dealing mainly in chemical products required for domestic cleaning and hygiene requirements. About 50% of the products are manufactured in-house and 50% of products are directly purchased from reputed manufacturers and traded under the brand name of VILLAHI. VILLAHI is a 100% family-managed organization with a total financial outlay of $500,000.0 for the setup.

The total revenue from operations including trading has been around $7,20,874.00 in 2011 compared to $655,089.00 of 2010 with an approximate 80% capacity utilization. The unit has a total of 15 employees working since the inception of the company and they are completely loyal to the organization.

 initial investment has been 100% from family members including the working capital, but over a period of time, the business has been self-sufficient in its financial requirements with profits and cash generated from operations.

The major raw material required for the manufacture of cleaning chemicals is from M/S Georgia Pacific, which is also the strategic partner in CCC operations. Another company, DROM supplies the essences for the cleaning chemicals. The entire value chain management is focused on optimizing revenues and margins; hence there is focused control on quality, cost, and delivery of Incoming supplies from different vendors. Since the available margins are due to severe competition in the market and a price-sensitive customer base, the cash flows are always under severe stress.

Organization

Vision: To be a market leader providing excellent customer service supported by the best in quality and to become a role model in the cleaning products market.

Mission: To be the most recognized enterprise at the local level known for its services with highly competitive prices and highly motivated workforce adding customer value to every operation

Objectives

1. To achieve a profit level of >30% in fast-selling chemicals and achieve a market share of >40% in five to ten of operations in the local markets.

2. To establish a strategic competitive advantage position for most of its products by focusing on strategies of low cost and differentiation in a span of the next five years.

Market Scenario

The market for cleaning chemicals is highly severe, volatile, and price sensitive. The competition is also led by product and service differentiation. There is heavy usage of advertising media such as TV, journals, magazines, direct e-mailers, brochures, free samples, etc.

Villahi does not have a separate marketing function, and the marketing is currently handled by a few employees who mainly handle sales and distribution logistics. Villahi, however, is planning to outsource its marketing function to an expert agency from outside on a contract basis.

The product mix for CCC is (1) institutional products, 10%; (2) hygiene products, 40%; (3) chemical products, 25%; general cleaning supplies, 25%. The sales are through distributors, and supplies are confirmed orders from distributors. The proximity to the US border further complicates the market with the influx of branded products from the United States. However, the strategic partnership with Georgia Pacific provides Villahi an edge over local competitors. In spite of the severe competition, Villahi has been able to achieve a 20% market share.

Villahi also has built a very strong brand image in a short span of over seven to eight years of its inception, especially with its products such as recyclable toilet paper and vegetable-coloured chemical products. In the absence of a thorough and organized market survey, the consistency in sales of different products gives the sense of confidence of sustainability of its market share. Each of the products gives a reasonable contribution in spite of highly competitive prices and severity of preference to quality and after-sales services of each of the players in this market. Villahi has already developed and supplied automatic dispenser systems to its customers, which are an edge in the hygiene products and better yield to its customers. However, there is a lot that needs to be done to improve after-sales services. Villahi at present has only record-based software on existing customers and receivable payments.

Manufacturing Strategy

Villahi so far has been completely dependent on the original process machinery installed in 2004 and has better profitably in view of the recovery of most of the depreciation from the investments. Villahi is planning to establish a subsidiary unit to manufacture specialized chemicals and products such as liquid soap dispensers, including grease removers, multiuse aromatizes, chlorine, muriatic acid, among others.

There is no established quality management system as a part of the manufacturing process. All special requirements of the customers such as chlorine levels etc., the same are supplied at better prices. The main quality problems are not with the main product but with the containers, which often leak and create customer dissatisfaction and irritation.

The main cost in addition to the product is the fuel, transportation, and employee pension schemes. Villahi is planning to modernize its manufacturing technology provided they are convinced of growth in the market for their products. They are also exploring opportunities to tie up with a Chinese enterprise for diversification of their operations.

Financial Performance

Major Operational Details	FY 2009–2010 ($)	FY2010–2011 ($)	FY2011–2012 ($)
Fixed assets	32,038	26,032	42,672
Current assets	56,656	69,065	108,110
Current liabilities	35,448	24,240	78,635
Gross working capital	53,247	70,858	72,146
Total gross revenues	586,000		720,874
Gross margins	37,037	17,611.10	17,392
Taxes	4,117.79	3,612.37	3,324
Gross depreciation	48,673	66,916	84,440
Net profit	37,038	17,611.10	17,392
Gross reserves	0	0	0

New Projects/Products (Investments)

We have a medium-term project to build a specialized chemical products factory, and to become a distributor for our competitors, with new process and automatic state of the art machinery. Any Specific issue/s concerning this area of business?

General Economic/Market Situation Influencing the Cash Flow Issues of the Organization

Overall enterprise economy depends greatly on the economy in our country, and the market has a strong growth potential due to the fact that our products are the first need for everybody. The cash flow problem is given for a policy of granting credit to our customers.

Marketing Function

1. Organizational structure for marketing function:

We don't have any organizational structure regarding marketing function; currently, we are evaluating hiring an outsourcing marketing professional to handle this aspect.

2. Product/services details (including product mix)

Institutional products, 10%
Hygiene products, 40
Chemical products, 25%
General cleaning supplies, 25%

3. We supply service, enterprises request an estimate for products, we do that, the purchase is authorized, and we deliver merchandize, afterwards we establish payment and collection with an enterprise collector.
4. Market details (including Original Equipment (OE), direct to market, spares, etc.).

Market segments Villahi supplies are rural, urban, agricultural, industrial, educational, defence, tourism, etc.

5. Market size (actual market share and market potential) for each of your major products is very wide, and it is not properly supplied in its whole; it exists one element that makes it more complex, which is the proximity to the US border. This makes the competition level complex. Villahi of Mexico participates with 20% of the total market quota in general; the growth is attributed to the alliance with the Georgia Pacific enterprise, which produces hygiene products.

6. Major competitors (product and segment wise)

Distribution channels: Wholesale and dealer network including logistics. Enterprise distribution channels are very important, and it is made by the enterprise delivering team, however, we have very good logistic around the city streets.

7. Brand image/equity of your products (any reliable survey report)

In spite of our short time in the market, our enterprise has a very good brand image due that we are a small local business, committed to the environment; one example is our toilet paper which is recyclable and the chemical product colours are from a vegetable source. Until today, we have not performed any evaluations to have indicators regarding marketing to know the Enterprise reliable level. However, the support and loyalty of our customers back us up.

8. Specific issues in this area: Product-related—price, quality, technology (product-functional), after-sales. Relation cost/benefit is very good for our enterprise, due that we handle high-quality products, good price, without being low, because, we have incorporated technology products such as automatic dispensers that impact the products yield for our customers, as well as the hygiene aspect, due that they don't have any contact with the integrated technology. We consider that service after the sale is deficient and this is an area to be improved in our enterprise.

9. Sales promotion/customers relations regarding this activity negotiations. Sales promotional/customer relations management activity—major aspects. The Villahi of Mexico enterprise has a type of CRM software, which works on customers relations to know consumption levels, prices, and a customer's credit record.

Case Questions

1. The entrepreneur would like to know, which are the alternative strategies that VILLAHI has to adopt in order to increase profitability level for the next three years?

2. Do you consider it is the right time for the management of Villahi to diversify into other business areas such as enterprises maintenance and hygiene services? Please, give us the bases and analysis for an expansion plan in our business (a business model).

3. How to improve our approach to customer services such that we retain loyalty and customer satisfaction despite fresh/feverish competition.

17

The BSNL Saga

A Case Study on the Ailing BSNL India's Public Sector Telecom Wing

Learning Objectives

What the financial liberalization norms and adopting principles of market economy and open to global competition can do to otherwise highly protected public sector units in India—perhaps Bharat Sanchar Nigam Limited (BSNL) is a glaring example of a failed enterprise getting exposed to global competition both in technology and marketing skills required and perennially becoming sick in spite of huge governmental support and involvement.

An industry that was used to unquestioned market leadership without any competition and its customers are tolerant to the dictator approach of the service provider having to wait decade long even to get a much-needed telephone connection was happy to welcome the reforms and getting rid of never compliant BSNL for their urgent business communications.

On several occasions, the government has poured in financial support to BSNL to manage its costs and expenses without the company waking up from its slumber of past glory and near-monopolistic behaviour.

It is really pathetic to see the lack of entrepreneurial spirit and fight for claiming its share in the ever-expanding telecom sector that BSNL today sees itself being maintained on ventilator support just capable of breathing and semblance of life. This case study is an opportunity for students of management to unravel real concepts of market economy and what is the real meaning of competitive strategies for survival and business sustenance.

Indian Business Case Studies. Varsha Parab, Ramesh Mahadik, and Diksha Tripathi, Oxford University Press.
© ASM Group of Institutes, Pune, India 2022. DOI: 10.1093/oso/9780192869432.003.0017

Synopsis

BSNL officers' group has warned that things may go out of hand, and the state-controlled telco would not survive for long unless the central government takes a decision on the telco's revival and facilitates a soft loan for capital as well as operational expenses.

'The situation is worsening and if a decision is not taken by the PMO, and a soft loan is not provided to meet Capex and Opex, BSNL will not last long. We have already apprised the concerned in Central Government of the situation', said Sanchar Nigam Executives' Association (SNEA) president Aftab Ahmad Khan. Khan further said that the BSNL officers had informed the country's top office about the situation which is deteriorating every passing day, and the decision-making within the government remains slow. The Department of Telecommunications (DoT), according to him, has also not even released a credit worth Rs. 3,300 crores since the Presidential Sanction it granted back in March this year, after the delayed salary disbursement for the first time.

Some of the executives' demands included allowing bank loan till the time of land monetization, allocation of 4G airwaves, and refund of access payment to the tune of Rs. 2,100 crores. The association also attributed bureaucratic hurdles leading to vendors outstanding worth Rs. 2,500 crores. More than 100 vendors including small-and-medium business owners, agitated at BSNL Delhi headquarters.

'We fully support BSNL executives' union. Since the rejuvenation plan has so far delayed, there is no option but to allow Rs. 6,000 crores to bridge funding to pay to operational creditors', Telecom Exports Promotion Council (TEPC) co-chairman Sandeep Aggarwal said, adding that salary payments alone couldn't make the telco survive.

Earlier, the Finance Ministry officials have opposed the voluntary retirement scheme (VRS) package worth Rs. 6,365 crores to BSNL and Rs. 2,120 crores to MTNL. However, the telecom department has been working on a slew of initiatives for BSNL revival that would require a Cabinet nod. Besides real estate assets monetization, the department is also looking to lease out towers, and fibre infrastructure which, according to analysts, could bring much-needed respite in a shorter term since land unfreeze may be dragged due to multiple policy challenges including the mutation process.

One of the proposals being considered by NITI Aayog, the government's policy think-tank, estimated BSNL's real estate at Rs. 1 lakh crore, fibre assets at Rs. 54,000 crores, and telecom towers at Rs. 29,000 crores. India's fourth-largest operator, according to industry statistics, has the lowest debt of close to Rs. 20,000 (Rs. 13000 crores) crores when compared to private sector rivals such as Vodafone Idea having Rs. 1.20 lakh crores, Bharti Airtel having Rs. 1.10 lakh crores, and Reliance Jio with Rs. 1.12 lakh crores worth of liabilities.

The Group of Ministers (GoM) headed by home minister discussed offering VRS and the fourth-generation or 4G airwaves to the stressed state-controlled BSNL and Mahanagar Telephone Nigam Limited (MTNL).

The sources aware of the development said that the group during the two-hour-long meeting discussed the ways to bring back the two public sector service providers back to health and considered monetization of land and building assets to fund VRS to the willing employees. The centre is also mulling operating synergy between BSNL and MTNL, to further save operational costs. MTNL offers cellular services in two metropolitans—Delhi and Mumbai, whereas BSNL operates in rest of the country. The revenue to wage ratio of both telcos, is much higher than those of private sector players.

Since 2016, both public sector operators have been demanding allocation of 4G radio waves to stay competitive in the data-led service delivery, which is also leading to their revenue fall on a quarter-to-quarter basis. The administrative cost for the allocation of 4G radio waves to BSNL is pegged at Rs. 14,000 crores.

The government also needs to immediately look at assets monetization strategies including towers and fibre to make BSNL stay afloat. The real estate assets, fibre optic network and mobile towers of BSNL are pegged at Rs. 1.10 lakh crores, Rs. 60,000 crores, and Rs. 35,000 crores tentatively. The proceeds can further be used to fund VRS, and 4G and 5G spectrum, as well as operational expenses of both telcos.

The Initiatives

BSNL begins land monetization, fair valuation at Rs. 20,000 crores. The public sector BSNL is in the process of identifying land parcels all over the country for monetization, which as per its internal estimate is valued at Rs. 20,000 crores in 2018–2019.

The state-run telecom major's corporate office has circulated a list of land parcels that are proposed for monetization through the Department of Investment and Public Asset Management (DIPAM) in the first instance. Time-bound monetization of land assets, mobile towers, and fibre networks will help BSNL earn some money in these tough times of falling revenues and rising losses. (However, it is understood that these land parcels are not completely free of encumbrances.)

'The total area of land parcels, which are spread across the country and have in-built structures, buildings and factories, is 32.77 lakh square meters (sq m) and the spare able land parcel is 31.97 lakh sq m', said an earlier BSNL corporate office letter to its circles seeking their comments.

The fair value of spare able parcel as on 1 April 2015, is Rs. 17,397 crores and the estimated present fair value of these lands is Rs. 20,296 crores. The enhancement in valuation is based on cost inflation index for FY 2014–2015 as 240 and FY 2018–2019 as 280.

'The valuation of these land parcels is proposed to be done along with the structures lying in the parcel after the in-principle approval for sale or long term lease by the government. The cost of buildings has not been included in the Fair Value of land parcels', it added. BSNL telecom has factories at Mumbai, Kolkata, West Bengal, Ghaziabad, Jabalpur, and wireless stations, as well as other offices and staff colonies have been included in the list of land parcels to be monetized. Some of these parcels are mutated, while some are not and the status of some of these parcels are freehold and some are on leasehold.

Struggling with poor cash flows from services and a severe financial crunch due to a huge workforce of 1.76 lakh (add 40,000 contract labour), BSNL is looking for non-core asset monetization under the broad policy of the government where DIPAM is the nodal department.

BSNL is expected to post losses of over Rs. 14,000 crores for the financial year 2018–2019, while its revenue is slated to be around Rs. 19,308 crores.

Salary expenditure is set to be a massive 75 per cent of the firm's total expenses at Rs. 14,488 crores. Its provisional loss in 2015–2016 was Rs. 4,859 crores, Rs. 4,793 crores 2016–2017, and Rs. 7,993 crores in 2017–2018. BSNL's loss is estimated to balloon to Rs. 14,202 crores in 2018–2019.

'Low tariffs due to fierce competition in the mobile segment, high staff cost and absence of 4G services (except in few places) in the data-centric telecom market are the main reasons for losses of BSNL.' In line with sector trends, BSNL has also seen a dip in its revenue after the entry of Reliance Jio in the market in 2016. The company's revenue is pegged at around Rs. 19,308 crores for 2018–2019, compared with Rs. 25,071 crores in 2017–2018 and Rs. 31,533 crores in 2016–2017.

The Government Is Planning a Revival Scheme for BSNL

The government is taking steps to make public sector BSNL more competitive and these include upgradation of technology and capital infusion. BSNL has inherited legacy issues and steps are being taken to make BSNL more competitive. 'To ensure stability in the Telecom sector, one PSU is very important,' it must be noted that India has the cheapest mobile and data rates across the world.

The government is considering capital infusion, including equity infusion in the public sector telecom company. The government is also working out the introduction of 4G services, after members expressed concern over the lack of technology upgradation by the BSNL. BSNL has to spend 75 per cent of its revenues on paying salaries to employees, while private companies have very low employee costs. BSNL has informed that there is no proposal to lay off over 54,000 employees.'

As per TRAI report, the total market share of BSNL is 10.72 per cent as on 31 March 2019, including 9.96 per cent in mobile wireless technology. However, stiff competition in the mobile segment, high employee cost, and absence of 4G services (except in a few places for BSNL in the data-centric telecom market is adversely affecting the competitive strength of BSNL.

Case Questions

1. It is often said that in India, 'The government has no business to be in business'. All exercises are done by several governments at the centre so far have not been able to see consistent success in the majority

of the PSUs. The main reason for not focusing on business credentials is perhaps the lack of push and follow-up from the professional business management approach even for survival, leave alone a growth strategy. Besides any action of turnaround or restructuring are considered detrimental to the government in ensuring success at the ballot box or alternatively, these are considered as potential opportunities to generate revenues for the government in terms of disinvestments and collecting huge funds for revenue generation targets to meet the government's budgetary commitments.

Do you think the current situation at BSNL is because of a lack of business acumen in running such companies in perennial distress?

2. The speed of technological disruption in the telecom industry is perhaps the severest amongst all industries in India and also in global markets. While private organizations are aware of the impact of disruptive technological changes, the government is not very sure of meeting such challenges by concerned PSUs. Hence allowing the technological obsolescence to worsen the distressing situations at PSUs such as BSNL, which has rendered the unit to be put on ICUs and Respirators.

How do you suggest The Governments come clean on such dubious distinctions in treating such ailing units as Cash Cows for disinvestment rather than successful businesses?

3. Do you see any turnaround strategy workable for BSNL? What areas do you think the government should focus on to avoid the closure of PSUs such as BSNL, and Air India story also perhaps falls under similar issues?

18

The 'Diesel Gate'

A Case Study on Volkswagen Scandal of Inserting a Cheat Device for Manipulating Emission Norms

Learning Objectives

This Case study tends to expose as to what business greed and extremely stringent compliance standards could collude to formulate a toxic heady idea of cheating the very crux of acceptance norms to help escape a bit more of hard work in sincerely walking the truthful way. This case study also briefly tries to unveil a few of the known facts about the German auto giant Volkswagen cheating and manipulating the emission norms on their vehicles for a singular objective of sustaining market share and improving revenues.

The students of management while studying business ethics may have quoted Germans as one community that swear by their honesty and sincerity of purpose in all that they do socially and business wise.

This is a bit difficult for the non-technical background students to understand the complicity of the topic and extent of involvement of the auto giant Volkswagen also known as 'Das Auto'. But the happenings as revealed so far are facts about a highly strategized deceptive approach adopted by the world famous company by exposing its dirty linen in public by being unceremoniously driven to culprit pedestal in the International Courts with no reasoning to put forth in their defence.

A great lesson to be learnt in business ethics and how carefully to avoid the temptations to slip badly to wipe out centuries old reputation of honesty and sincerity.

Indian Business Case Studies. Varsha Parab, Ramesh Mahadik, and Diksha Tripathi, Oxford University Press.
© ASM Group of Institutes, Pune, India 2022. DOI: 10.1093/oso/9780192869432.003.0018

Synopsis

The 'Diesel gate' scandal was suppressed for years—while we should have been driving electric cars.

But that was not how it turned out. They chose a Volkswagen Jetta as their first test subject, and a Volkswagen Passat next. Regulators in California agreed to do the routine certification test for them, and the council hired researchers from West Virginia University to then drive the same cars through cities, along highways, and into the mountains, using equipment that tests emissions straight from the cars' exhausts.

It was clear right away that something was off. At first, German wondered if the cars might be malfunctioning, and he asked if a dashboard light had come on. That didn't really make sense, though—the cars had just passed the California regulators' test. His partners thought there might be a problem with their equipment, and they recalibrated it again and again. But the results didn't change. Nitrogen oxide (NOx) pollution from the Jetta's tailpipe was 15 times the allowed limit, shooting up to 35 times under some conditions; the Passat varied between five and 20 times the limit. German had been around the auto industry all his life, so he had a pretty good idea of what was going on. This had to be a 'defeat device'—a deliberate effort to evade the rules.

'It was just so outrageous. If they were like three to five times the standards, you could say: "Oh, maybe they're having much higher NOx emissions because of the high loads"', or some other external factor. 'But when it's 15 to 30 times the standards, there is no other explanation', he says. 'It's a malfunction or it's a defeat device. There's nothing else that could possibly get anywhere close'.

German wasn't ready to level such a serious accusation against a huge company such as Volkswagen, so he kept quiet while the research moved forward. Much later, his boss was surprised to learn how early he had suspected the truth. 'He said: "You knew there was a defeat device? Why didn't you tell me?"' The answer was simple. 'We're an $8m organisation. VW could have squashed us like a bug'.

German and his colleagues pressed ahead with their work and, when the study was finished, they posted it online. That was May 2014. He was still nervous, so the council didn't issue a press release, nor did the report name the manufacturer. As a courtesy, he sent a copy to someone he knew at Volkswagen, noting 'by the way, Vehicles A and B are yours'. German's group also forwarded the findings to the US Environmental Protection Agency (EPA) and California's Air Resources Board (Carb). 'We were definitely scared. We wanted EPA and Carb to take over'. After the results were posted, he would email the agencies now and then. No one replied, and having spent more than 13 years at the EPA himself, he knew what that meant.

The regulators were investigating. And while they struggled to determine what was causing the discrepancy between pollution in the lab and on the road, Volkswagen executives quietly debated their next move. After months of foot-dragging, Volkswagen promised to remedy the problem, which it blamed on a technical glitch. It began recalling cars, updating the software in hundreds of thousands of them.

Months later, California ran new tests. Emissions were still far over the limit. Now regulators wanted to see the software controlling the vehicles' pollution systems. And they made an extraordinary threat to get it: if Volkswagen did not turn over the code, it would not get the approvals it needed to sell cars in California and a dozen states that used its standards. The EPA threatened to withhold certification for the entire US market. 'That,' German says, 'was when VW came clean'.

Case Details

Dieselgate, as it became known, exploded into one of the biggest corporate scandals in history. Over almost a decade, Volkswagen acknowledged, it had embedded defeat devices in 11 million cars, mostly in Europe, but about 600,000 in the United States. The software detected when emissions tests were being run, and pollution controls—components inside the engine that reduce emissions, sometimes at the expense of performance or fuel consumption—worked fine under those circumstances. But outside the lab, the controls were switched off or turned way down, and NOx levels shot up as high as 40 times the legal limit. With mind-boggling gall, Volkswagen had even used the software update it was forced to carry out to improve cars' ability to detect when they were being tested.

And, as it turned out, Volkswagen wasn't the only one evading the law. Less flagrantly, but to similar effect, the vast majority of diesel cars were making a mockery of emissions rules. In the wake of the revelations in the US, European governments road-tested other big brands too.

In Germany, testers found all but three of 53 models exceeded NOx limits, the worst by a factor of 18. In London, the testing firm Emissions Analytics found 97% of more than 250 diesel models were in violation; a quarter produced NOx at six times the limit. 'As the data kept coming in, our jaws just kept dropping. Because it is just so systematic, and so widespread', German says. 'VW isn't even in the worst half of the manufacturers.' With a few honourable exceptions, 'everybody's doing it'.

In the United States, where only around 2% of cars are diesel, the rule-breaking had an impact. But the health consequences have been far more severe in Europe, where drivers had been encouraged for years to buy diesel cars—when the scandal broke, they accounted for more than half of all sales. In 2015 alone, one study found that failure to comply with the rules caused 6,800 early deaths. To put it more plainly, tens of thousands of people had died because carmakers felt so free, for so long, to flout the law.

Of course, the painful light cast by the scandal didn't just expose corporate wrongdoing. It also made visible a failure that is just as distressing. Across Europe, including in Britain, governments responsible for enforcing the law and protecting their people's health had utterly neglected to do so. The fact of the matter, German explained to me, is that European air quality regulators don't have the muscle or the resources their US counterparts have long possessed. European countries have never built the enforcement capability needed to give teeth to pollution rules. Governments, he says, 'don't seem to be able to do anything about it, in most cases don't even seem to want to do anything'.

Air Pollution Hanging over London

While the US is, in so many ways, an environmental laggard compared to Europe, air quality is a glaring exception. The EPA has, over the years, built up tremendous legal and technical expertise. At least until its evisceration in the Trump years, the EPA was known for its diligence in supplementing regulations with circulars and advisories that precisely defined every term, clarifying ambiguities, and laying out what was allowed and what was not. The result was a system that, if not watertight, was a lot less leaky than elsewhere. In Europe, while the rules might look similar, no one goes to the trouble of making clear exactly what they mean, so polluters provide their own interpretations. Its atrocious air offers a cautionary tale that those undermining the US regulation would do well to heed.

How could this have happened in countries that are among the wealthiest in the world, on a continent whose name is a byword, elsewhere, for environmental progressivism?

It starts with an enforcement structure that almost seems designed to let violators through. The European Commission sets the rules on how much pollution a car is allowed to produce. But the job of enforcing them falls not to Brussels, but to national governments. And a car company preparing to release a new model can choose which country certifies it; every EU nation must then honour the approval. A savvy carmaker opts for a place where it provides lots of jobs, where officials are likely to be pliant.

The national enforcement agencies, for their part, are generally under-staffed, poorly funded, and lacking in technical expertise. Britain is an exception, but in most nations, these weak agencies don't even test cars themselves. About a dozen individual vehicles must be checked before a new model is approved, and the tests are often run by outside contractors. When they are done, the manufacturers hand the paperwork to regulators, and the results, says Mock, are usually accepted with little question.

What's more, the specifics of the tests—speed, acceleration and so on—are publicly available. So, a manufacturer can build its cars to produce little pollution under those particular conditions and a lot more the rest of the time.

There is another route those companies take: programming pollution controls to turn off when the weather is too hot or too cold, when a car is just being started or is speeding up or slowing down or climbing a hill—conditions they frame as extraordinary, but account for a big chunk of driving time. If challenged, the companies can cite a legal loophole, claiming the switching off is necessary to protect engines.

Now, at last, European regulators have begun requiring cars to be tested on the road, not just in the lab. But the real problem, to my mind, is even bigger: it seems clear that the flaws in European nations' enforcement are more fundamental than the particulars of one testing method. The problem is the system itself, which is riddled with weakness and ripe for abuse. Politicians have begun, post-Dieselgate, to tighten it, but it remains a system designed under the gaze—and the lobbying pressure—of a powerful industry.

So, Germany knew. Perhaps other governments did, too. Many of its people, though, did not, certainly didn't know. Nor did the buyers of millions of diesel cars. Nor the hundreds of millions of people who breathe the air they taint, trusting for so long that companies were following the law—and that governments would catch them if they didn't.

The diesel cheating scandal is in some sense a failure of innovation—yet another symptom of carmakers' desire to stick with what they know, with the cars that reliably deliver profits. That caution is surely at the root of why European manufacturers pushed governments looking to shrink carbon footprints to turn to diesel, rather than, for example, hybrids such as those that Honda and Toyota had already put on roads by the late 1990s. With their vast resources and the marketing muscle to bring consumers along, who knows what Volkswagen and the others could have come up with. We have all paid the price for their decision not to try.

Case Questions

1. What in your opinion really prompted a 'touch me not' quality and performance-based business culture of the Germans so obviously admired by even competitors for its rigid compliance to standards to so surreptitiously resort to the cheat device only to be caught napping by the world at large?

2. How will the German government and its people treat this issue and what steps they would take retrospectively to at least help correct this sudden disgraceful incidence and tarnished reputation of being one of the most admired countries adhering to par global standards in product and service quality?

19

Domino's India Supply Chain Management

A Case Study on Supply Chain Management

Learning Objectives

The main learning objective of this case study is to study the components of the supply chain of a fast-food company and its effective management with special reference to Domino's Pizza. This case also focusses on competitive analysis in the pizza sector, especially the competition between Domino's and McDonald's. To study the different logistics models for improving the overall business is also one of the objectives of the case.

Synopsis

In the view of business expansion, Domino's revamped its supply chain operations in India. Initially, Domino's had a simple logistics model. The case discusses the various benefits of the new logistics model and discusses the reasons for the revamp. The benefit of low costs achieved through the new model was passed on to the customers in the form of lower prices. The case also compares Domino's new supply chain model with McDonald's supply chain model.

Introduction

In early 2000, Pawan Bhatia (Bhatia), the CEO of Domino's Pizza India (Domino's), was a man in a hurry. Ever since Bhatia took over as the CEO

Indian Business Case Studies. Varsha Parab, Ramesh Mahadik, and Diksha Tripathi, Oxford University Press.
© ASM Group of Institutes, Pune, India 2022. DOI: 10.1093/oso/9780192869432.003.0019

of Domino's in November 1999, he had been frantically reworking the pizza chain's India strategy. Bhatia was planning to open 150 new outlets by the end of 2002, covering 23 cities including Bhubaneshwar (Orissa) and Jamshedpur (Bihar). In late 1999, Indocean Chase, the private equity fund, bought a 25% stake in Domino's operations in India from the Delhi-based industrial family, the Bhartias, who held Domino's franchise in India. Domino's told investment bankers at the fund that it planned to go in for an initial public offering (IPO) in the next two years. Indocean Chase advised Domino's to go beyond its 16 outlets in Delhi to exploit the potential in the pizza delivery business. Unless a well-thought-out expansion plan was put into place, the IPO was unlikely to find too many takers.

As part of its expansion plans, Domino's revamped its entire supply chain operations, from sourcing raw materials to shipping them for processing at a central location to delivering it to the customers. Initially, Domino's had a simple model. It had three self-contained commissaries in New Delhi, Mumbai, and Bangalore, which bought their own wheat, tomatoes, and other ingredients, processed them, then delivered them in refrigerated trucks to each outlet. However, volumes were expected to increase when Domino's planned to open new outlets. Therefore, the existing model had to be revamped. Bhatia said, 'It's crucial for us to build a low-cost supply chain operation which takes costs out of the system and in turn gives us greater pricing flexibility in the marketplace.' Analysts felt that Domino's had to rethink its supply chain operation because it was the biggest area of costs. Since 75% of Domino's customers ordered either from office or home, it did not have to lease large plots of land in prime locations to attract traffic. Instead, it needed an efficiently managed call centre to bring better returns. In the late 1950s, Dominick De Varti (Varti) owned a small pizza store named Domi Nick's Pizza on the Eastern Michigan University campus in Ypsilanti, Michigan. In 1960, two brothers who were students of the University of Michigan—Thomas S. Monaghan (Thomas) and James S. Monaghan (James)—bought the store for US$900. In 1961, James sold his share of the business to Thomas.

The pizza business did well and by 1965, Thomas was able to open two more stores in the town -Pizza King and Pizza from the Prop. Within a year, Varti opened a pizza store in a neighbourhood town with the same name, Domi Nick's Pizza. Thomas decided to change the name of his first store, Domi Nick's Pizza, and one of his employees suggested the name

Domino's Pizza. The advantage of this name Thomas felt was that it would be listed after Domi Nick in the directory. Domino's philosophy rested on two principles—limited menu and delivering hot and fresh pizzas within half an hour. In 1967, it opened the first franchise store in Ypsilanti, and in 1968, a franchise store in Burlington, Vermont.

However, the company ran into problems when its headquarters (the first store) and commissary were destroyed by fire. In the early 1970s, the company faced problems again when it was sued by Amstar, the parent company of Domino Sugar, for trademark infringement. Thomas started looking for a new name and came up with Red Domino's and Pizza's Dispatch. However, there wasn't any need for it because Domino's won the lawsuit in 1980. In 1982, Domino's Pizza established Domino's Pizza International (DPI) that was made responsible for opening Domino's stores internationally. The first store was opened in Winnipeg, Canada. Within a year, DPI spread to more than 50 countries and in 1983, it in-augurated its 1,000th store.

Around the same time, new pizza chains like Pizza Hut and Little Caesar established themselves in the United States. Domino's Pizza faced intense competition because it had not changed its menu of traditional hand-tossed pizza. The other pizza chains offered low-priced breadsticks, salads, and other fast food apart from pizzas. Domino's faced tough competition from Pizza Hut in the home delivery segment also. Little Caesar was eating into Domino's market share with its innovative marketing strategies. By 1989, Domino's sales had reduced significantly and cash flows were affected due to the acquisition of assets. In 1993, Thomas took measures to expand Domino's product line in an attempt to revive the company and tackle competition. The company introduced pan pizza and breadsticks in the United States. In late 1993, Domino's introduced the ultimate deep dish pizza and crunchy thin crust pizza. In 1994, it rolled out another non-pizza dish—buffalo wings. Though Domino's did not experiment with its menu for many years, the company adopted innovative ways in managing a pizza store.

Thomas gave about 90% of the franchise agreements in the United States to people who had worked as drivers with Domino's. The company gave ownership to qualified people, after they had successfully managed a pizza store for a year and had completed a training course. Domino's also gave franchises to candidates recommended by existing fran-chisees. Outside the US, most of Domino's stores were franchise-owned.

Domino's was also credited for many innovations in the pizza industry and setting standards for other pizza companies. It had developed dough trays, corrugated pizza boxes, insulated bags for delivering pizzas, and conveyor ovens.

In 1993, Domino's withdrew the guarantee of delivering pizzas within 30-minutes of order and started emphasizing on Total Satisfaction Guarantee (TSG), which read: 'If for any reason, you are dissatisfied with your Domino's Pizza dining experience, we will re-make your pizza or refund your money'. Domino's entered India in 1996 through a franchise agreement with VamBhartia Corp.

In Delhi, with the overwhelming success of the first outlet, the company opened another outlet in Delhi. By 2000, Domino's had outlets in all major cities in India. When Domino's entered India, the concept of home delivery was still in its nascent stages. It existed only in some major cities and was restricted to delivery by the friendly neighbourhood fast-food outlets. Eating out at 'branded' restaurants was more common.

To penetrate the Indian market, Domino's introduced an integrated home delivery system from a network of company outlets within 30 minutes of the order. Goutham Advani (Advani), chief of marketing, Domino's Pizza India, said, 'What really worked its way into the Indian mind set was the promised 30-minute delivery'. Domino's also offered compensation: Rs.30 off the price tag if there was a delay in delivery. For the first four years in India, Domino's concentrated on its 'Delivery' strategy.

Domino's Logistics Model

Analysts felt that Domino's took a cue from McDonald's supply chain model. However, they opened that the level of complexity in McDonald's system in India was not as high as that of Domino's. Commented Bhatia, 'McDonald's operations are not as spread out as ours. They are in four cities while we are in 16. Centralizing wouldn't work on such a geographical scale'. The logistics model adopted by Domino's offered some obvious benefits including lower transportation costs, cheaper procurement, and economies of scale. Domino's had already cut out the duplication in procurement and processing of raw materials across each of the three commissaries.

The old model of self-contained commissaries had another disadvantage: adding new outlets did not translate into greater economies of scale. Bhatia planned to extend the model to other parts of the country as well. The commissary was to be located near the largest market in that region. Bhatia said, 'Our roll-out began only after we mapped out our procurement strategy'. Based on the agricultural map of India, Domino's looked at McDonald's had one of the best logistics models in India. To maintain consistency and quality of its products, McDonald's shipped all the raw materials lettuce, patties et al to a cold storage close to the main market. Based on a daily demand schedule that was prepared a day in advance, the required amount of raw material was transported to individual outlets.

For ensuring the best product at the lowest cost. The inputs like, tomatoes would come from Bhubaneshwar, spices from the south, baby corn from Nepal (where it's 40% cheaper than in India), and vegetables from Sri Lanka. Similarly, Domino's India planned to extend its operations to Nepal, Sri Lanka, and Dhaka. The company planned to establish a commissary in Sri Lanka, Domino's also identified specialty crops in each region. The commissary in that region was entrusted with the task of processing that specialty crop. For instance, the commissary for the eastern region in Kolkata was responsible for buying tomatoes, processing them, and then sending them to all the other commissaries. Similarly, the northern commissary had to deliver pizza bases. This way, Domino's minimized duplication as well as the dangers of perishability. Once the new model was formalized, Bhatia planned to use Domino's 25 refrigerated trucks.

To transport products for other companies on the same route. For instance, if an operator in Kochi (Kerala) needed to transport specialty cheese, he could use the Domino's fleet to transport his products. Said Bhatia, 'Not too many people have refrigerated trucks in the country. And we can offer them quality service because we will be giving them standards, we use for ourselves'. Company sources said that enquiries from clients for such transport facilities had started coming in. Bhatia said he was in the process of selecting a person to head the logistics operation, which would be spun off as a separate profit centre. Bhatia seemed confident that the profit centre had the potential to bring in Rs 10 billion by 2006. However, he said the profit centre would not be allowed to impede the growth of the pizza business, Domino's core operation. Only those deliveries that did not delay or de-route the truck would be considered.

Domino's hoped to lower its prices by saving from the logistics model and third-party transportation. In April 2000, Domino's announced a cut in pizza prices to Rs 49. Domino's was also targeting large corporate offices, railway stations, cinema halls, and university campuses for faster growth. It had already established an outlet at Infosys corporate office in Bangalore and at three cinema halls—PVR in Delhi, Rex in Bangalore, and New Empire in Kolkata. Domino's also classified its outlets into superstores, express stores, and regular stores.

Superstores were those which generated high traffic and therefore had more counters than the regular outlets (the outlet in Churchgate, Mumbai). Express stores were those where people were expected to walk in and order rather than ask for home delivery (university campuses, offices, or cinema halls).

Conclusions

Managing logistics and operations in a business is highly crucial to ensure that the company meet out the necessities and requirements of consumers on a regular basis. As in this case, we understand the need and importance of Domino's new model of supply chain in India and how and why it is compared with McDonald's supply chain model. In the future, Domino's will have to focus more on its supply chain management as the number of its branches and overall business is increasing in India. They have to increase their operational efficiency and purchasing process.

Case Questions

1. Briefly explain the need for Domino's to revamp its supply chain operations in India?

2. What are the benefits Domino's derived after the revamp?

3. Compare the supply chain models of Domino's and McDonald's. Which model is superior and why?

20

Low-Cost Disruptive Strategy

A Sustainable Disruptive Strategy in Indian Aviation Industry—A Case Study on IndiGo Airways

Learning Objectives

To critically analyses the low-cost competitive advantage as also a disruptive strategy to effectively achieve market leadership status. To understand various costs and challenges faced by the aviation industry of India. This case can be used for Post Graduate and Undergraduate management students to analyse as to how IndiGo airlines succeeded in a highly competitive Indian aviation market and improve its market share and profit by adopting a highly cost-sensitive 'low-cost' disruptive and competitive advantage strategy.

Synopsis

With the liberalization of the Indian economy and the adoption of the open-sky model helped the civil aviation industry to grow in India. Civil aviation in India had gone through three major stages. First, where government-led Air India dominated the market, then in 1991, after liberalization, private players like Jet Airways, Kingfisher Airlines, Air Deccan, and Sahara Airlines took the market over Air India; this was the time when civil aviation was considered to be luxury and consumer were ready to high prices and avail high-grade services. From 2005 onwards entry of low-cost carriers changes the entire airways market.

Indian Business Case Studies. Varsha Parab, Ramesh Mahadik, and Diksha Tripathi, Oxford University Press.
© ASM Group of Institutes, Pune, India 2022. DOI: 10.1093/oso/9780192869432.003.0020

IndiGo Airways entered the Indian market with a full long-time strategy and opting blue ocean strategy. India is the ninth-largest civil aviation market in the world which is expected to grow and become the third-largest by the year 2030. Liberalization geared the growth of the civil aviation industry in India. This case talks about the strategy of 'low-cost fares' introduced by 'IndiGo' in the Indian market, which has been successfully adapted by the Indian market and growing in terms of customer base. This case analyses various strategies used by IndiGo airline to minimize is cost to work on margins and which made them the market leaders over the previous several years

Case Details

Among various segments of passengers, IndiGo targeted the middle class and lower-middle-class segment. Several other companies entered the market on the same line, successfully capturing the market share from the market giants leading to big losses for existing leaders. The growing income in the hands of the middle class has given a boost to the aviation industry in India. Statistics of the Indian Aviation industry had 183.90 million passengers in the year 2017–2018 in comparison to 158.43 million in the year 2016–2017, which is growing. IndiGo is a market leader in the civil aviation industry of India, acquiring approximately 44% domestic passenger market share. This case analyses which airline had maintained its low cost successfully and dealt with micro- and macro-level economies impactful.

The aviation industry in India is going through a roller-coaster round; some are earning profits and some are facing losses are fighting to survive in spite of the growing market. The price war among these companies is putting great pressure on survival. Big companies like Kingfisher, Sahara, Jet Airways had fallen in the past few years for different reasons few most important reasons for these air crafts were the services provided, airfare, fluctuating oil prices. Aviation companies like IndiGo, AirAsia, SpiceJet entered the market with the strategy of introducing low-fare travel, which attracted the market share very fast. The market, which was dominated by Kingfisher, Air India, and Jet Airways slowly shifted towards IndiGo, SpiceJet, low-fare airlines. These new entrants understood the sentiments of the market and successfully entered the market. Another reason for losses in the aviation industry is increasing fuel charges, where all the airline companies are fighting to survive. Most popularly, to safeguard from price fluctuations of international oil pricing, hedging is used. To a major extent, it is successful. But again, it depends on the financial condition of airline companies how well they are capable of adjusting hedging in their balance sheet. Aviation Industry consists of various organizations involved in the manufacturing of aircraft, airline flying, maintenance, operating staff, training centre, and other regulatory authorities like airports, DGCA, etc. 'Low cost' concept was introduced in the year 1995 by the UK and Ireland, launching easyJet and Ryanair by using South West model. This strategy was successful and encouraged the low-cost airline industry.

History of Indian Aviation

The history of the aviation industry in India started before independence; first airmail service was launched in India for 10 km distance between Allahabad and Naini during the Kumbh Mela of 1911 on a Humber bi-plane. In 1912, Indian Air services, in collaboration with UK-based Imperial Airways, launched a service between Karachi and Delhi. It was an extension of London–Karachi flight of Imperial Airways.

In the year 1915, Tata & Sons launched regular airmail services between Karachi and Madras. The next major step taken in the aviation history of India was in 1932 when Tata Airline launched its first commercial airline under JRD Tata. Hindustan Aeronautics Limited (HAL) was founded in 1940 by Walchan Hirachand in association with the then-Mysore Government in Bangalore. In the year 1945, 'Deccan Airways' was founded by Tata and Nizam of Hyderabad and in 1946, Tata Airlines changed its name to 'Air India', and by 1948, Air India started international flights under the name of 'Air India International'.

In the year 1953, Air Corporations Act was passed by establishing 'Indian Airlines' and 'Air India International' by merging eight airlines of that time Deccan Airline, Airways India, Bharat Airways, Himalayan Aviation, Kalinga Airline, Indian National Airways, Air Services of India, and Air India. In 1972, 'International Airports Authority of India' was launched. In 1981, 'Vayudoot Airlines' was launched, many changes in the aviation industry were seen till 1990. The year 1990 was a milestone in Indian aviation history when the government of India decided to introduce private players in the market in the form of charter and non-scheduled services under 'Air Taxi' scheme. The effect of liberalization in this segment resulted in attracting new private investors to invest in this sector; in 1991, Sahara Airline was introduced, which later merged with Jet Airways as JetKonnect. In 1993, Jet Airways started its operations, then in the year 2005, Go Air and SpiceJet became operational. In the year 2006, IndiGo was launched by Rahul Bhatia and Rakesh Gangawal, the year 2013 Air Costa and in the year 2015, Vistara Airlines entered the market. Vistara Airlines is a joint venture between Tata Sons and Singapore Airlines. Jet Airways, Kingfisher Airlines, and Air India had been the luxury airlines with high-cost premium quality service to customers; they approached high-income group as customers. Whereas SpiceJet, IndiGo, and Vistara entered the market by stretching the market segment and making it more approachable to the middle class.

IndiGo Airlines

IndiGo Airlines started in the year 2006 as a private company owned by Rahul Bhatia of InterGlobe enterprise and Rakesh Gangwal, an ex-chairman and CEO of US Airways, United States-based NRI. Rahul Bhatia convinced Rakesh Gangwal to partner in this venture, who was initially hesitant to enter the aviation industry due to the heavy risk involved. Finally, he agreed, and Rahul Bhatia's InterGlobe has a 51.12% stake in IndiGo, and Rakesh Gangwal's Caelum owns 47.88% (Virginia-based Company). Since its inception, IndiGo had concentrated on being a low-cost carrier, and it focussed mainly on:

> Offering low fares
> Being on time
> Delivering a courteous and hassle-free experience

Promoters of IndiGo opted for the blue ocean strategy where they analysed the Indian market and crafted a specific place for them that was untouched by existing players in the market. Rahul Bhatia and Rakesh Gangwal had the experience of airline industry they analysed the need of time-bound low-fare market with no-frills required to enter the Indian airspace when competitors in the market were competing for the experience of flying with high cost, IndiGo planned to bring airline services from class to mass, opted for reducing the overall cost of an airline Services.

Before entering the market, Rahul Bhatia & Rakesh Gangwal ordered 100 A320 Airbus from Hamburg, Germany on 16 June 2005 in Paris Airshow. The president of Airbus and CEO, Noel For geared, praised the airline before its operations started 'Indigo is the result of extensive analysis and planning by very experienced airline executives and we are convinced it will be a successful new player in a market that is both large and fast growing'. IndiGo's purchase of 100 aircraft was well strategized; it ensured low operating cost, latest aircraft technology, full maintenance support from Airbus, and comfort in Airbus to fight with the competitors in the market having leased aircraft, old aircraft which consumed high fuel. This bulk order provided an edge of low-cost carrier and long-term maintenance relationship with Airbus and reduced the training cost of its employees from ground to onboard staff.

Finally, IndiGo Airlines was launched on 4 August 2006. At this, another visionary step taken by promoters was to acquire parking space on main hubs Mumbai and Delhi. By the time they announced operations, they were ready with a schedule of the first 20 aircraft. They decided to add a plane every six weeks, which helped to gain flyers of Kingfisher; IndiGo was ready to absorb spillover traffic of Kingfisher better than Jet Airways, which was leading the market.

IndiGo visionaries believed in working on margins to support the low-cost fare strategy, and it was tuff to earn profit in the initial four years as ticket prices were approximately 40% of the cost of operations. IndiGo opted for a low-cost single-class model with no-frills. It decided to provide on-time good services with the least cancellation. IndiGo tried to minimize its turnaround time by controlling many small-level activities. It kept a lean structure of workforce where Rahul Bhatia met personally once each employee was appointed for IndiGo.

Minimizing Turn Around Time

It opted for the strategy of managing small jobs like loading, unloading, cleaning, etc., to reduce the turnaround time. They have a record of a 14-minute turnaround time. Training of staff is done in a manner where time management is kept on utmost importance; IndiGo deplane passengers in approximately 6 minutes, unloading of baggage takes approximately 10 minutes which gives them a benefit of least turnaround time of 23–25 minutes, whereas the industry average is of approximately 30 minutes Which helps them to fly 12 hours in a day in comparison to 8–10 hours of others. It provides a **single service** of economy class with no-frills provided on board. It does have its onboard sales facility 'Hello 6E' and beverages are also sold on flight. IndiGo's

Tag Line: Go IndiGo
Headquarters: Gurgaon, Haryana
Marketing Highlights:

6E the airline code: the airline has code 6E, which can be heard during shopping in flight as 'Hello 6E', which sounds like 'Hello Sexy'
On the doors leading to cockpit states 'Flying is serious profession'

Tongue-in-Cheek Advertising Strategy

USP: Low Cost, Single Class, On-time model with no-frills attached.
IndiGo Airlines had taken strong and well-planned long-term initiatives since its inception to reduce the fare prices and maintain the quality.

Competitive Strategies of IndiGo

Single Fleet

IndiGo has A320-232, A320-214, A320-271N in its fleet of aircraft in the year 2017–2018. By the start of the year 2019, IndiGo had a fleet of 220 aircraft including 74 new-generation A320 NEOs, 130 A320 CEOs, 15 ATR, and 1 A321 NEO. By the year 2017–2018, IndiGo and competitor owned aircraft details are as under:

Aviation Company	No. of Aircraft
IndiGo	162 Aircraft + 10 ATR72
Jet Airways	113
Air India	136
SpiceJet	58

Using a single type of aircraft reduced the training and maintenance cost on employees and aircraft. The employees once trained can easily work on the aircraft of airways. It has tie-up with Air France for holding inventory of components which relaxes IndiGo from bookkeeping.

Sale and Leaseback Model

This model allows to sell an asset and leaseback for a long term, which allows continuous usage of the asset without owning generally applied on fixed assets like land or capital goods like trains and aeroplanes. This helps in removing debt from the balance sheet of the airline. To negotiate the volatile environment, this extra income was a well-executed plan of low-fare airlines. It has a great demand in the market as Neos uses less fuel by 15% than most of the aircraft.

Minimizing Turnaround Time

IndiGo opted for strategy of managing small jobs like loading, unloading, cleaning, etc. to reduce the turnaround time. They have a record of 14-minute turnaround time. IndiGo deplaned passengers in approx. 6 minutes, unloading of baggage take approx. 10 min. Cleaning takes approx. 5 min. and the aircraft is ready to board, which gives them a benefit of least turnaround time of 23–25 min, whereas industry average is of approximately 30 minutes. Which helps them to fly 12 hours in a day in comparison to 8–10 hrs. of competitor airlines.

Lean Work Force

IndiGo maintains a lean workforce and tune them perfectly with the vision of the airline, which makes employees taking responsibility of their work. Rahul Bhatia meets every employee selected from crew to ground staff.

RNP Approach

RNP is required navigation performance approach; it provides precise onboard navigation performance monitoring and keeps a check on navigation accuracy by timely informing any deviations found. It helps to make a safe landing at tuff destinations also. It ensures aircraft stays in a specific containment area. It allows the airline to fly between two 3D points on a defined path. It provides path to fly over terrain like mountains of the Himalayas at lower levels to avoid bad weather as well as over the open oceans and remote locations. Alaska Airlines was the first airline in 1996 to use RNP approach. It enhances the performance and accuracy of airlines.

RNP helps in navigating more direct routes near the destination airport, which helps in reducing the fuel cost and faster turnaround from airports. The use of new aircraft reduced their maintenance cost in comparison to the competitors who were using old aircraft, which needed expenses and time on maintenance.

Route Planning (Hub and Spoke Model)

IndiGo has expanded its destinations in the market gradually and went for opting for secondary airports to lower the cost and increase the customer base. IndiGo generally picks profitable routes, in spite of having more fleet count than competitors, it prefers specific destinations which are popular and with prime time. Any new route selected would have more than two destinations.

Branding

It never desperately advertises to sell its seats. IndiGo can establish itself in the target market successfully.

Various small pocket savings and lucrative offers were provided to the customers.

- ✓ **Prom:** Stands for IndiGo promise, which charges Rs. 49 as a fee for refund in case of late or cancelled flights, etc.
- ✓ **Flexi fares:** Provides facility to make unlimited changes in travel dates without any extra charges.
- ✓ Collaborating with various payment modes like banks, MobiKwik, Airtel, etc. provides easy and extra savings to customers.

Tongue-in-cheek advertising: This type of advertisement makes customers remember the advertisement for a longer duration.

Use of technology: Use of better technology when other airlines are using manual link system; IndiGo uses digital link system for transmission of messages between the aircraft and ground staff in a short and simple manner via aircraft communications addressing and reporting system (ACARS). Which automatically triggers messages from aircraft to the operations control centre at departure and landing, which automatically records time and time can be easily monitored.

Fleet planning: IndiGo believes in retaining younger flights in order to avoid heavy maintenance costs, thus it phases out aircraft before its mandatory time, generally six to eight years.

Fuel management: IndiGo has the lightest passenger seat of 12.8 kg and paint covers weight less than 50 kg overall. Keeping the lower weight saves fuel costs. IndiGo chose V2500 engines to cut fuel burn of almost by 2%. Many such initiatives are taken to reduce fuel costs.

Fuel Hedging: The government has allowed fuel hedging in India. IndiGo could manage its profit by efficient management of fuel prices and fluctuation in the value of rupee.

Managing Working Capital

Working capital is required for any company to run its day-to-day business; it consists of current assets minus current liabilities. Generally, a positive working capital is considered to be the perfect one but, in some cases, where cash is taken before service organizations even can manage to avail benefits from negative working capital, which helps them to run business on suppliers' and customers' money and reduces the burden of loan.

Future Plans of IndiGo

IndiGo is looking forward to long-haul international flights in order to keep the fares low. IndiGo flies to 52 domestic and 16 international destinations. IndiGo has a total 53 domestic and 17 international destinations. They fly to Athens, Budapest, Brussels, Tel Aviv, Malta, Paris, Dublin, Copenhagen, Prague, Vienna, Zurich, and Amsterdam. They also fly for 12 code share destinations beyond Istanbul on Turkish Airlines.

John Nair, head (business travel) Cox & Kings, says, 'IndiGo's plans to launch an LCC model for long-haul flights will be received quite enthusiastically. The return fare on economy class to most European capitals from Mumbai are close to Rs. 50,000 plus and goes up during the holiday season. If an LCC can offer direct connectivity for a basic fare of Rs. 25,000 with additional top ups for meals, baggage and blankets, which further takes the fare to, say, Rs. 35,000, it is still a value deal. Indian customers will lap it up.'

The plans to go for long haul can be facing problems of aircraft acquisition cost where IndiGo is planning to acquire Airbus A330neo wide-body jets and high fuel prices. About 15% of its daily flights are for overseas in the year 2018, it got permission to fly for London, Madrid, and Paris.

This data shows all their aircraft are of Airbus, which is a renowned name for new technology and comfort. IndiGo continuously upgraded the process to give better services at a lower cost. IndiGo changed its training from role-specific to one central operation in three segments—for specific roles, functional skill training, coaching for customer service, and soft skills and leadership training. Leadership training was given to promote ownership in every employee towards customers, which would help in enhancing long-term customer relations. Its training and employee management strategy was successfully operational. From 2008 to 2015, IndiGo was recognized as 'Great place to work in India' and Aon's best employer for the year award was received in the year 2016–2017. IndiGo provided a ramp to enter the aircraft, which provided ease to kids, old aged, and physically challenged customers. To save the time of aircraft and customers on the counter, IndiGo provided hand-heled scanners to the ground staff for fast checking of the customer with hand baggage. Domestic airline demand had grown to 117.04 billion of the year 2017–2018 from 98.64 billion of the year 2016–2017. The domestic air capacity is as follows:

	2016–2017	2017–2018
Domestic passenger	103.75 M	123.3 M
International passenger	54.68 M	60.58 M
Total passenger base	158.43 M	183.90 M
Domestic airline demand (RPK)	98.64 B	117.04 B
Domestic airline capacity (ASK)	116.95 B	134.54 B

Source: http://www.dgca.nic.in/

Note: ASK is calculated as the sum of products obtained by multiplying the total number of seats that are available in each flight stage by the corresponding stage distance. RPK is calculated as the sum of the product obtained by multiplying the number of revenue passengers carried on each flight stage by the corresponding stage distance. (Data taken from DGCA website.)

As per the data of DGCA, the controlling authority of the aviation sector in India, the data of passenger growth for Jan–March 2019 shows growth of 4.92% from the corresponding period of the previous year. IndiGo Airlines was ready to capture the market since its inception.

	Market Share as per Demand	Market Share as per Passenger Carrier	Year
IndiGo	40.9%	39.7%	2017–2018
Jet Airways	14.6%	15%	2017–2018
Air India	12.2%	12%	2017–2018
SpiceJet	12.3%	13.1%	2017–2018

Source: http://www.dgca.nic.in/

The number of passengers grew to 125.08 lakhs in January 2019 from the corresponding period of January 2018 being 114.65 lakhs, a growth of 9.10% is reflected.

Year on Year Comparison of Number of Scheduled Domestic Passengers and Passenger Load Factor (PLF)

Name of the Airline	PASSENGERS (in Number)			PLF (%)		
	2016–2017	2017–2018	YoY Growth (%)	2016–2017	2017–2018	CHANGE (+/–)
Air India	1,37,34,192	1,47,55,383	7.4	79.2	80.5	1.3
SpiceJet	1,32,36,143	1,61,30,815	21.9	92.9	94.7	1.8
Jet Airways	1,62,76,098	1,85,50,776	14.0	81.8	84.3	2.5
IndiGo	4,16,00,088	4,89,55,983	17.7	85.2	88.2	3.0
GoAir	86,45,969	1,08,29,141	25.3	88.0	88.6	0.6

Source: DGCA.

IndiGo Airlines was able to keep its strong foot in the volatile aviation market of India. This can be clearly seen in their financial results. Analysing the results of competitors in the year 2017–2018.

Airline	Operating Revenue	Operating Expenses	Operating Results
Air India	28,596.10	2,15,615.9	2,980.20
Jet Airways	2,12,576.65	2,12,070.03	506.62
SpiceJet	61,912.66	58,465.90	3,446.76
IndiGo	1,85,805.00	1,68,897.04	16,907.96

Source: DGCA.

IndiGo has done an excellent job in understanding these needs and has devised its strategy in a manner to fulfil most of these. Well-planned strategies are paying in terms of IndiGo showing ten consecutive years of profitable operations. It has acquired 43.4% of the market share by February 2019.

Costs and Challenges Involved in Airline Industry

Cost

The cost involved at various levels needed to be studied at this stage.

Fuel cost: The first and largest operational cost for an airline is its **fuel expense** and expenses related to its oil procurement. It is observed that when the prices of oil increase, the share prices of airline industry fall, and when the prices of oil decrease, the share prices of airline industry fall. Any airline must make reserves for oil and to safeguard from future fluctuations of prices, hedging is very important. Hedging is done around the world by all the airline companies to cope with oil and its related uncertainties. The Indian airline industry has a very less inclination towards hedging oil prices; the comparatively lower ratio makes tuff for them to face the price fluctuation jerks of oil (data).

Rental of flight equipments: Airline companies lease aircraft in order to reduce the cost of buying aircraft and increase the temporary capacity of airlines. The data states by October 2018, IndiGo had 144 leased aircraft, Jet Airways had 106 leased aircraft, Air India had 87 leased aircraft, SpiceJet had 58 leased aircraft. IndiGo and Jet Airways had 47% of total leased aircraft functioning in the market. Fifty-four percent of total leased aircraft is utilized by low-cost airline operators.

General and administrative charges like **airport charges**, which are paid by any airline company to the airport as landing charges and take-off charges. The airline must pay for the flights standing at the airport, for flying and landing from the respective airport. The frequency of flights helps to reduce this burden on the airline.

Flight crew salary and expenses costs that are onboard pilot, stewards, and airhostess, who are on the board with passengers.

Flight equipment maintenance and overhauling cost
User charges
Ticketing and sales promotion
Depreciation and amortization

Taxes and pax service to be paid to the government.

Major Challenges Faced by IndiGo

IndiGo as India's largest budget airline, had shown a quarterly loss of Rs. 652.13 crores in September (Q2) 2018 in comparison to Rs. 551.56 crores a year ago; it was its first loss since going public. These losses were majorly due to an increase in total expenses, which grew 58% higher in Q2, fuel expenses raised to 84%, which led to foreign exchange loss of Rs. 335.4 crores. The loss was even due to the grounding of A320Neo due to Pratt and Whitney engine issues in 2017, which has not impacted its flight operations but impacted finance. IndiGo had 40 A320Neo planes, 11 were grounded due to P&W engine issues after a series of shutdowns in mid-air, which impacted its 1.08 lakh passengers. The airline had to cancel approximately 84 flights at that time. IndiGo and other airlines are facing a price war of fares in the market which is slowly denting their profits.

Crazy tax rates levied by the government still considering the airline business as a luxury mode of transportation is burdening the load of airlines. Regulators and government's disinclination to revive this least regulated market which spreads ambiguity of future in front of these airlines.

Case Questions

1. How do you correlate concepts of low-cost competitive strategy with ground-level developments for IndiGo Airlines?

2. As on recent survey, most of the low-cost airlines have been reporting steep fall in passenger load and huge debts accumulated on repayments for lease amounts of aeroplanes which are forcefully grounded for lack of demand. How do you explain this situation when a low-cost strategy was intended to increase market share and better earnings from operations?